# A Doctor on the California Trail

A Docto

*The Diary of Dr. John Hudson Wayman
from Cambridge City, Indiana, to the
Gold Fields in 1852*

# on the California Trail

### Edited by EDGELEY WOODMAN TODD

OLD WEST PUBLISHING COMPANY / Denver, Colorado

*Copyright 1971*

*Old West Publishing Company*

ISBN 0-912094-16-8
LIBRARY OF CONGRESS NUMBER 72-162933

ALL RIGHTS RESERVED — PRINTED IN UNITED STATES OF AMERICA

*Gold-fever! A malady*

*for which there is no cure . . .*

Frank Waters, THE WILD EARTH'S NOBILITY

# Contents

| | |
|---|---|
| viii | Locations on Wayman's Trail |
| ix | Illustrations |
| xi | Foreword |
| 1 | Introduction |
| 25 | Diary of Dr. John Hudson Wayman |
| 27 | March 25 – April 30, 1852 |
| 30 | May 1 – May 31, 1852 |
| 43 | June 1 – June 30, 1852 |
| 62 | July 1 – July 31, 1852 |
| 78 | August 1 – August 31, 1852 |
| 90 | September 1 – September 30, 1852 |
| 98 | October 1, 1852 – March 25, 1853 |
| 111 | Letters of Dr. John H. Wayman to Dr. James V. Wayman |
| 125 | Bibliography |
| 133 | Index |

# Locations on Wayman's Trail

*Beginning with St. Louis*

| | |
|---|---|
| St. Louis   April 4–6, 1852 | Bear River   July 1 |
| Lexington   April 13 | Soda Springs   July 4 |
| St. Joseph   April 17–22 | City of Rocks   July 12 |
| Camp   April 23–30 | Humboldt River |
| Little Blue River | Big Meadows   Aug. 1 |
| Fort Kearny   May 19 | Carson Pass   Aug. 23–24 |
| Ash Hollow   May 28 | Placerville   Aug. 27 |
| Courthouse Rock   June 1 | Stockton   Aug. 31 |
| North Platte River | Sonora   Sept. 1 |
| Fort Laramie   June 5–6 | |
| Independence Rock   June 16 | |
| South Pass   June 22 | |
| Big Sandy | |
| Green River | |

# Illustrations

xiii     Doctor Wayman's Medical License

xvi     Dr. John Hudson Wayman

21     Margaret Ormsby Wayman

25     Doctor Wayman's Diary

MAPS

6     The Doctor's Trail to California

17     Southern Mines

# Foreword

FEW PEOPLE IN THE UNITED STATES were unaffected by the discovery of gold in California in 1848. From all parts of the nation and from all walks of life, thousands hurried to the Mother Lode country expecting to reap financial benefits. Among them was the author of this diary, Dr. John Hudson Wayman, a young medical doctor who left his home in Cambridge City, Indiana, in the spring of 1852 bent on reaching California by the overland route.

Before leaving, he bought a medical pocket book for $2.00 and two diaries costing forty cents each. If he ever used the second diary, which seems unlikely, neither it nor the medical book has survived. The diary in which he recorded the details of his journey and his experiences for several months in California is like many which other emigrants carried, although those I have examined vary in size. Wayman's measures five by three and a quarter inches and is bound in magenta-dyed leather. The back cover extends around the right side, and a tongue slips under a narrow strip of leather on the front cover to keep the book closed. Not including end sheets, the diary consists of one hundred twenty leaves with twenty-one horizontal blue lines per leaf, each with marginal red stripes, now faded. A leather-lined pocket is attached to the inside of the back cover.

Wayman filled the book to capacity. He even wrote diary entries and made notations on the end sheets as well as on the inside of each cover. In addition, he filled two loose slips of paper with brief entries; folded in half, they measure four by five inches. Inserted in the pocket of the diary at a later time by a member of the family are six letters which Wayman wrote to his brother, Dr. James Vallores Wayman.

Wayman used pencil when he wrote the diary as well as the letters, and for the most part he wrote legibly. In view of the fact that the diary is, at the present writing, one hundred seventeen years old, the manuscript is still remarkably clear and is smudged in only a few places. Occasionally a word or phrase is illegible.

In preparing this edition, I have tried to reproduce what Wayman actually wrote and have duplicated his errors in spelling and punctuation as well as other irregularities. The most difficult problem has been to determine when he intended to write capital letters. In many instances, his intention is unmistakable; in many others it is borderline. I have often had to make arbitrary decisions, realizing that his meaning did not depend upon capitalization. The same is not true, however, with regard to punctuation. Wayman did not distinguish consistently between periods and commas, and sometimes a short horizontal stroke substitutes for them or is intended as a dash. Meaning does in some instances depend upon interpreting what he meant by certain hastily-written marks. If a down stroke is clearly a comma, even where a period would normally be used, I have usually let it stand.

The history of the diary after it passed from John H. Wayman's hands following his death is unknown in precise detail. It is at present owned by Fred A. Rosenstock of Denver, Colorado, who purchased it from Mrs. Wayman E. Ballenger of Concord, California. Mrs. Ballenger's late husband, Wayman Ezra Ballenger, was the grandson of Dr. James Vallores Wayman (a brother of John) and the son of his daughter Elizabeth, who married William Elmer Ballenger. Elizabeth's twin brother, John Vallores Wayman, remained a bachelor and took pride in preserving the family keepsakes. During the last two years of his life (he died on December 8, 1929), he made his home with Mr. and Mrs. Wayman Ballenger in California and handed on the articles he had preserved to Mrs. Ballenger's husband. Among them was John Wayman's diary.

In editing the diary I have kept a number of objectives in mind. One has been to reproduce the text as accurately as possible. In addition, I have tried to identify events and places as well as clarify allusions which the reader might not recognize. In this book, as well as in others which I have edited, it has seemed imperative to examine the physical setting and to orient myself in relation to its topography. As a result, some of the information in this edition is based upon a personal knowledge of much of the route over which Wayman actually traveled toward his destination. During a period of many years, I have enjoyed the pleasant avocation of trail hunting and have walked in the very ruts of the emigrants' wagons, have photographed their inscriptions on sandstone bluffs, and have sought out their campsites and even their burial spots. Vivid in my memory is the time when I turned over a flat rock and found the name of an emigrant who had been buried there. Before undertaking the actual work of editing Wayman's diary, I knew I must once again return to the old trail and seek out the places that he saw.[1]

---

[1] For detailed topographic features of the terrain Wayman covered on his way to California, see the National Topographic Maps, 1:250,000-scale series, prepared by the Geological Survey. An index is available.

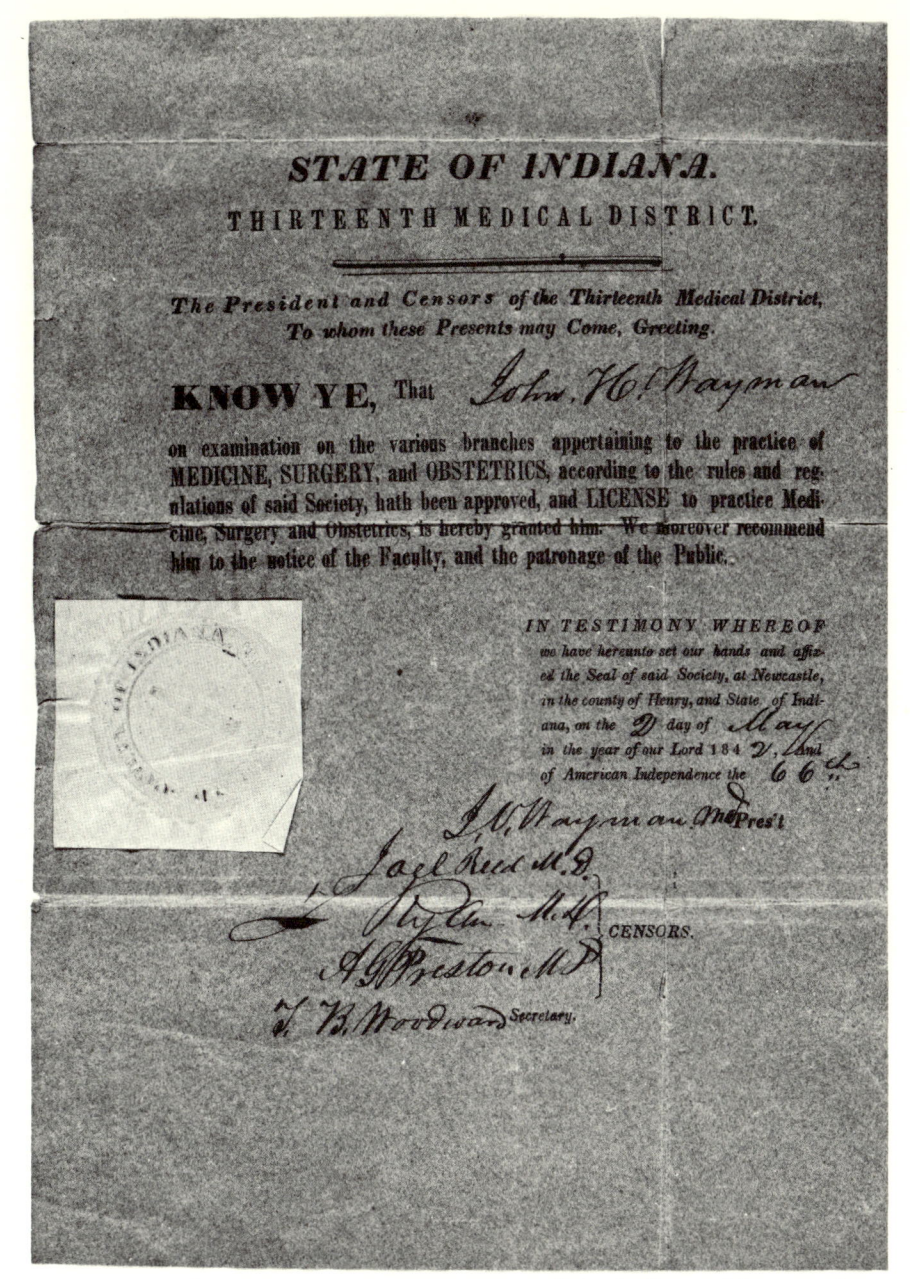

DR. WAYMAN'S MEDICAL LICENSE, granted in Indiana, May 2, 1842.

I began at the Green River north of Kemmerer, Wyoming, and tried to determine where he might have crossed the river. From there I worked west in an effort to cover as much of his actual route as is accessible today by automobile. Only in this way can one obtain a visual knowledge of the valleys, rivers, and mountain passes that Wayman knew and thus recognize the accuracy of what he recorded in his diary. He saw snow, for example, on the Humboldt Mountains on July 17, 1852; I saw snow on the same mountains and from the same spot on July 15, 1968.

Moreover, editing Wayman's diary seemed to provide an opportunity to look at the 1852 migration in a broader human context than the pages of the diary alone give us. With this in mind, I have turned to other 1852 diaries, especially those in the Bancroft Library at the University of California in Berkeley, and drawn upon them to supplement Wayman's. Through a reading of over a hundred diaries of that year, I have been able to develop some sense of what it was like to be an emigrant in 1852.

And finally, since this is the diary of a man about whom little is known and about whom nothing has been written, I have included in the introduction as much biographical information as presently-available sources make possible. Hopefully, one can thus see the diary in relation to the life of a pioneer physician in mid-nineteenth century.

In preparing his diary for publication, I have obligated myself to several institutions and to many people. No book like this is solely the work of one person, regardless of what the title page may say. I wish, therefore, to express my sincere thanks to James de T. Abajian, former librarian of the California Historical Society who, upon learning of my undertaking, voluntarily communicated with me and offered his knowledge; to Mrs. Wayman E. Ballenger, former owner of Dr. Wayman's diary, who has graciously answered my questions about the Wayman family and has put at my disposal valuable material which would otherwise have been unobtainable, including the photograph of Margaret Ormsby Wayman; to Mrs. Marion H. Bates, Assistant Librarian, Ohio Historical Society; to Robert H. Becker, Assistant Director of the Bancroft Library, who generously put the resources of that great institution at my command and who has replied to numerous letters requesting information I did not have; to Colorado State University for a research grant which funded a trip over Wayman's trail to California and for a leave of absence to work on this book; to Mrs. Robert M. Conner, President of the Ohio Genealogical Society; to W. N. Davies, Jr., Chief of Archives, State of California, for furnishing information about the early licensing of physicians in that state; to Ronald DeWaal, Humanities Librarian, Mrs. Loretta V. Saracino, Inter-library Loan Services, and to other members of the staff of Morgan Library of Colorado State University; to Mrs. Rawlins Dexter, for typing the manuscript; to Mrs. Dugdale of the California State Library at Sacramento, who placed before me several 1852 diaries and other materials of the period which I would not otherwise have known about; to Mrs. George W. Eastman of Oakland, California, who generously shared her knowledge and patiently

# FOREWORD

answered question after question about the Southern mining district and persons connected with it; to Carlo M. De Ferrari of Sonora, California; to Miss Mary Isabel Fry, Reference Librarian, Henry E. Huntington Library, who, as she has so frequently in the past, made the incomparable resources of that institution available to me; to Dale L. Morgan of the Bancroft Library, who helped immeasurably in directing me to 1852 diaries and other materials there; to Miss Myrtle T. Myles of the Nevada Historical Society, who furnished information about Mrs. Wayman and her first husband, Major William Ormsby, and events connected with them; to Miss Thelma G. Neaville, Librarian, Marysville City Library, Marysville, Californa; to Miss Annette Osmundsen of the Morrison-Reeves Library, Richmond, Indiana, who furnished information about Wayman's brother Dr. James Vallores Wayman; to Fred A. Rosenstock, close friend, bibliophile, publisher, and present owner of Wayman's diary, who made this book possible; to Silas E. Ross and Grover W. Russell for information about Wayman's association with Free-Masonry; to Mrs. Virginia Rust, Assistant in Manuscripts, Henry E. Huntington Library, who placed before me the 1852 diaries in its collection, one of which was the longest and most valuable of any I read; to Miss Verla M. Stinson, Recorder, Ormsby County Courthouse, Carson City, Nevada, for supplying a copy of John and Margaret Wayman's marriage certificate; to Mrs. Walter T. Swingle of the Library of the California Historical Society, who befriended me beyond the call of duty and even furnished a free lunch in the kitchen of the Society's old mansion; to Lois J. Todd, who helped make the working typescript of the diary and who rendered valuable editorial assistance; to Thomas R. Wayman of Cambridge, Ohio, whose interest in his family's genealogy led me to information that I would probably not otherwise have found; to my friend Frank Waters, of Taos, New Mexico, who granted permission for me to use the quotation from his novel *The Wild Earth's Nobility* as an epigraph; and finally to Merle W. Wells, Historian and Archivist, Idaho State Historical Society, to whom I have incurred a debt of gratitude now for three books. To all these persons, I warmly express my appreciation for their contributions to this edition of Wayman's diary.

EDGELEY WOODMAN TODD

Fort Collins, Colorado

DR. JOHN HUDSON WAYMAN. From a small photograph made in San Francisco in 1865.

# Introduction

## I.

ON THE MORNING OF JANUARY 24, 1848, James W. Marshall found gold in the tail race of the sawmill whose construction he was supervising for John Sutter on the south fork of the American River in California. By this discovery, he unknowingly determined the destiny of countless numbers of persons — Dr. John Hudson Wayman among them — and altered the course of American history.[1]

The impact of Marshall's discovery was immediate. By the end of the following summer and fall, a rush had started from all parts of California as well as from Oregon, and fortune hunters arrived daily from places as distant as Mexico, Chile, Australia, and even China.[2] Soon the news reached eastern parts of the country, and by late summer, 1848, the press began publishing reports of the gold finds. Interest intensified during the winter, and President Polk's annual message to Congress on December 5, 1848, reinforced the growing excitement. When, just two days later, actual samples of the precious metal itself were displayed in the nation's capitol, the effect was instantaneous and profound. Paper after paper proclaimed the news in extravagant phrases: "The Eldorado of the old Spaniards is discovered at last," wrote the New York *Herald;* in the opinion of the Pittsburgh *Daily Dispatch,* "An emigration will immediately commence for which we venture to say no parallel can be formed in history."[3] The sensational news from the west coast spread from one section of the East to another until the whole country was astir with exciting rumors of instant

---

[1] An account of his discovery appears in *James Marshall, the Discoverer of California Gold,* by Theressa Gay, pp. 145–51. See also John W. Caughey, *Gold is the Cornerstone,* Chapter I. Facts of publication for these and all other references appear in the bibliography.

[2] Ralph P. Bieber, "California Gold Mania," *Mississippi Valley Historical Review,* XXXV, 12–13. See also Caughey, pp. 23–24. Some of these "forty-eighters" made impressive finds. One of them found $20,000 worth of gold in six weeks. Others took from $800 to $15,000 every day from the north fork of the American River (*ibid.,* p. 29). Chapter II in Caughey gives additional information about the "forty-eighters."

[3] Quoted by Bieber, "California Gold Mania," p. 21.

wealth. From the United States the rising gold fever spread to Canada and even leaped the Atlantic to Europe. The contagion was international.[4]

The winter of 1848-49 gave people of adventurous spirit time to prepare for crossing the wide stretches of the continent or for making the journey by sea — discussing routes, laying in supplies, mortgaging or selling land, buying wagons, securing passage. Some even pawned valuable possessions to obtain money for the venture.[5] Those who chose the overland route had to wait until the weather became favorable for wagon travel in the spring. Thus it was not until April or May, 1849, that individuals, families, and organized companies began congregating at the supply points and jumping-off places along the Missouri River.

Of the many who set out early in 1849 was Alonzo Delano, whose physician recommended the trip as a means of improving his health. What he tells us at the beginning of his journal, one of the best of many accounts kept by gold seekers, suggests how individuals responded to the forces luring them westward. He says, for example, that "About this time, the astonishing accounts of the vast deposits of gold in California reached us, and besides the fever of the body, I was suddenly seized with the fever of the mind for gold; and in hopes of receiving a speedy cure for the ills both of body and mind, I turned my attention 'westward ho!' and immediately commenced making arrangements for my departure."[6] When he engaged passage on a steamer going up the Missouri, he found as he says, "Nearly ever State in the Union . . . represented."

Travel to California was not new, but the increase in the number who went there in 1849 as compared to 1848 was fifty-fold.[7] The non-Indian population, to look at this influx another way, increased from 14,000 in 1848 to 223,000 or more towards the end of 1852, the year that Wayman arrived there.[8]

The rush for gold that began in 1848 and 1849 continued in 1850, declined in 1851, and then increased in 1852. As more and more people joined in the adventurous challenge to reap a harvest of wealth, every class of society from the high to the low was affected. In Bancroft's words, they included "the trader . . . , the toiling farmer, whose mortgage loomed above the growing family, the briefless lawyer, the starving student, the quack, the idler, the harlot, the gambler, the hen-pecked husband, the disgraced . . . the many earnest, enterprising, honest men and devoted women."[9] He might also have added the physician.

---

[4] See *ibid.*, pp. 3–28, for a richly documented account of the spread of the "gold fever."

[5] *Ibid.*, p. 23.

[6] *Across the Plains and Among the Diggings* (1936), p. 1. Delano's account was originally published in 1854.

[7] George R. Stewart, *The California Trail*, p. 217.

[8] Rodman Paul, *California Gold*, p. 25. See also his *Mining Frontiers of the Far West, 1848–1880*, p. 15.

[9] Quoted in Caughey, *Gold is the Cornerstone*, p. 45.

# INTRODUCTION

## II.

IT IS NOT SURPRISING, consequently, that two of the Wayman brothers, James Vallores and John Hudson Wayman, both of them physicians, should have decided to give up their practices in Indiana and join in the general exodus to the California El Dorado. First to go was James, who left home in the fall of 1849. Taking the Panama route, he arrived in San Francisco on the *Sea Queen* early in January, 1850, and went directly to the southern mines near Sonora and later to the northern mines above Marysville. When he became discouraged by conditions at both places, he returned to Indiana in 1851 or 1852 and resumed his medical practice.[10] However disappointing his experiences in the gold fields may have been, they were not sufficient to deter his brother John from venturing there in 1852.

Of Dr. John H. Wayman's early life before he went to California little has been preserved. One of six children, he was born in 1820 on a farm near Covington, Kentucky, the son of Moses and Ruth (Jones) Wayman.[11] The family moved to Henry County, Indiana, in 1829. James, after studying medicine with a Dr. Joel Reed, received an M.D. degree in 1837 from Ohio Medical College in Cincinnati, where he had studied under Dr. Samuel Gross,[12] one of the outstanding American physicians and surgeons in the nineteenth century.[13]

Medical education in the United States during the first half of that century, when medical schools were on an insecure footing and often short-lived, was vastly different from what we have become accustomed to today. Standards were low, diagnosis and treatment of disease were far from scientific, and unbelievable chicanery was commonplace. There is the case, for example, of a medical quack in the California gold fields whose sole knowledge of medicine, if it can be called

---

[10] This information comes to me from Mrs. Wayman E. Ballenger of Concord, California, whose late husband was the grandson of Dr. James V. Wayman.

[11] Covington is located across the Ohio River directly below Cincinnati in Kenton County, Kentucky, on the Licking River. According to Estelle C. Watson in *Some Martin, Jefferies, and Wayman Families*, p. 144, Wayman was born in Campbell County, Kentucky. Information that he was born near Covington comes from Mrs. Wayman E. Ballenger.

Wayman's father was born on May 11, 1785, probably in Culpeper County, Virginia. His parents were Herman and Elizabeth (Clore) Wayman. In addition to John, the other children of Moses and Ruth Wayman were James Vallores (b. October 14, 1811), Milton Herman (b. 1813), Moses (b. 1815), William (b. 1817), and Elizabeth (b. 1833). See Watson, p. 144.

[12] *History of Wayne County*, II, 605. Xerox copy furnished by Annette Osmundsen of the Morrison-Reeves Library, Richmond, Indiana, January 23, 1969.

[13] Dr. Gross was the author of *Treatise on the Anatomy, Physiology, and Diseases and Injuries of the Bones and Joints* (1830), a notable book in its field, followed by others of great distinction. See *Dictionary of American Biography*, VIII, 19. Dr. James Wayman thought so highly of Dr. Gross that he named his first son, Willard Gross Wayman, in his honor.

that, came from boatmen and fishermen whom he knew as a boy living along the Tennessee River.[14]

In contrast, Wayman's training was fortunately of a superior kind. When he was preparing for his career, medical education in Ohio and Indiana was dominated by the preceptoral system. Sometimes a medical student's training was limited entirely to this method, based as it was upon a practicing physician's transmitting his knowledge to his protégé working alongside him. In other instances, a student would put in two or three years of such work and then supplement it by study in a medical college, from which he would graduate with his M.D. degree.[15]

John Wayman's decision to enter medicine may have been influenced by his brother's example. In all likelihood, he first studied under a preceptor (as James had done) before entering the Cincinnati College Medical School, where Dr. Samuel Gross was then Professor of Pathology, Physiology, and Jurisprudence.[16] The eminence of this physician and teacher indicates that the education the Wayman brothers received was of high quality by the standards of the time.

Wayman graduated with the M.D. degree in 1841 or 1842 and received a license on May 2, 1842, to practice in Indiana. This license, which still survives and is herein reproduced, bears the signature of his brother, president of the Thirteenth Medical District of the State of Indiana. What definite qualifications Wayman had to meet to obtain his license are obscure. In contrast to standards in Ohio, where a physician had to present credentials of a fairly high caliber, standards in Indiana were lax. The state legislature in 1825 and in 1829 had authorized the Indiana State Medical Association to grant licenses, but the law neglected to prescribe qualifications or even to provide penalties if a physician practiced without one.[17] But as a graduate of a medical school with a good curriculum,[18] Wayman would have been able to satisfy any requirements that may have been expected of him, and his license shows that he was examined in the practice of medicine, surgery, and obstetrics. Taking everything into consideration, his preparation was in all probability as good as he could have received in the region, and when he followed the lure of gold and adventure to California in 1852, he was better prepared than many, if not most, of the doctors who went there.

All such practitioners, however, regardless of the quality of their training, were seriously limited in their knowledge of the causes of disease. The germ

---

[14] Richard Dunlop, *Doctors of the American Frontier*, p. 178.

[15] Burton D. Myers, *The History of Medical Education in Indiana*, pp. 6–7. See also Emma Lou Thornbrough, *Indiana in the Civil War Era, 1850–1880*, p. 532.

[16] See Francis R. Packard, *History of Medicine in the United States*, II, 797.

[17] Thornbrough, *Indiana in the Civil War Era*, pp. 533–34.

[18] At the Cincinnati College Medical School the curriculum consisted of anatomy, pathology, physiology, surgery, obstetrics and the diseases of women and children, materia medica, the practice of medicine, chemistry, and botany (Packard, *History of Medicine . . .* , II, 797).

theory, the work of Louis Pasteur, would not be formulated until many years later. In 1852 the causes of cholera, for example, the most dreaded and deadly scourge of the overland emigrants, was still not understood, although the experience of some physicians on the trail led them to believe that contaminated drinking water might be responsible.[19] Lacking scientific knowledge of the causes and cures of many ailments, doctors who struck out across the country, as Wayman did, resorted to a common body of nostrums: bleeding, purging, sweating, blistering, homeopathy, water cures, and numerous others.[20] There is no evidence to show what kinds of treatment Wayman offered his patients while he traveled to California, but he was probably no exception in applying those just enumerated.

### III.

IN DECIDING TO VENTURE TO CALIFORNIA, Wayman was doing what thousands of other people in his region were doing. I do not have the figures for the number who left Indiana, but it has been estimated that from the neighboring state of Ohio somewhere between 13,000 to 15,000 were already in California by 1852.[21] It must, indeed, have been difficult to resist the spirit of the times — the onward surge to the west coast that reminds one of nothing so much as the great migrations of lemmings in their headling plunge to the sea. Robert Glass Cleland has stated that during the years following Marshall's discovery of gold, the human migration to California ". . . was so stupendous as to out-rank in point of numbers anything of its kind in the nation's history, and to stand on an equal footing with some of the great world movements of population."[22]

Exactly what motivated Wayman to go there remains obscure. Adventure, ambition, the chance of gaining wealth in the gold fields must have been dominant. Too, he was still young — only 32 in 1852 — and uncommitted with family responsibilities. Something of what was in his mind is suggested in a letter he wrote to his brother James two years later: "I think that a voluntary exile of 3 years is sufficient to satisfy any reasonable appitite [sic] for the New, strange and marvelous — I am well pleased . . . with my tour to California, and hope to profit by it through all coming life. A ramble of this character is not time

---

[19] Dunlop, *Doctors of the American Frontier*, p. 100, tells of a Dr. John Powell who came to this conclusion. He urged emigrants to keep water pure and encouraged them, when it was not otherwise available, to dig into the ground until they struck water.

[20] George W. Groh, *Gold Fever*, pp. 8–9.

[21] Melvin R. Thomas, "The Impact of the California Gold Rush on Ohio and Ohioans." Master's thesis, Ohio State University, 1949, p. 46.

[22] *History of California*, p. 232.

OVERLAND ROUTE OF WAYMAN PARTY
FROM ST. LOUIS TO CALIFORNIA

Soda Springs
July 4

Bear River
July 1

Big Sandy

Independence Rock
June 16

South Pass
June 22

Fort Laramie
June 5–6

Courthouse Rock
June 1

Ash Hollow
May 28

Fort Kearny
May 19

St. Joseph
April 17–22

Camp
April 23–30

Lexington
April 13

St. Louis
April 4–6, 1852

lost to a close observer, aside from money matters[.]"[23] In any case, his decision to go west determined the course of the remaining years of his life.

That decision made, he departed from Cambridge City, Indiana, on March 25, 1852, leaving behind him his relatives (including his mother, who was still living) and a house on which he owed money. With him was Elbridge Vinton, but whether Vinton was also bound for California is uncertain. Going south to Cincinnati, Wayman boarded the steamer *North Star* and sailed down the Ohio and up the Mississippi to St. Louis, arriving there on April 4.[24]

St. Louis that spring was filled with the bustle of emigrants scurrying to obtain supplies and make arrangements for passage up the Missouri River to various jumping-off points. Arriving in St. Louis a little later that same month, John H. Clark, headed as Wayman was for the gold country, wrote in his diary that "... all was hurry and confusion; horses, drays, mules, carts, merchandise, white men and negroes filled the entire space between the landing and the first row of buildings. How or in what manner a person was to make his way through such a medley was not easily explained."[25] Wayman managed to secure passage on the steamship *Clipper No. 2* and on April 17, eleven days later and 500 miles from St. Louis, disembarked at St. Joseph, Missouri,[26] an important starting point and outfitting post for the 1852 migration.

Somewhere between Cambridge City and St. Joseph, he had joined with a small group of men to form a party — perhaps by pre-arrangement, perhaps not — which eventually consisted of seven or eight persons, including Wayman himself and Elbridge Vinton (assuming that he still remained). These persons were a guide, whose services were probably secured in St. Joseph; a minister, who remains nameless; Maston Campbell, who went along as cook; William Loring, otherwise unidentified; a man named MacPherson, usually referred to in the diary as Mac; and someone named M. Shearer, who might have been the guide. Since the party was small, they could get along with a few horses and one light cart drawn by oxen. They crossed the Missouri on April 23, remained in camp

---

[23] Letter to Dr. James V. Wayman from Forest City, California, June 12, 1854. Doctors who took the trail to the gold fields were probably motivated by as many reasons as laymen. One physician from Ohio, Dr. David Maynard, left home because of a sharp-tongued wife and a debt of $30,000 (Dunlop, *Doctors of the American Frontier*, p. 102). Most doctors were probably less interested in practicing medicine than in gaining wealth and then returning as soon as possible to their homes. Often they did not practice their professions at all but engaged in mining or in other menial tasks. See J. Roy Jones, *Memories, Men and Medicine*, pp. 1–2.

[24] Cabin fare in 1849 was $7.00 (Joseph E. Ware, *Emigrants' Guide to California* [1932 reprint], p. 3). It may have been increased by 1852.

[25] "Overland to the Gold Fields," *Kansas Historical Quarterly*, XI, 230.

[26] Cabin fare for one passenger from St. Louis was $6.00 in 1849, according to Ware, *Emigrants' Guide*, p. 2.

# INTRODUCTION

on the west bank until the first day of May, and then started their great trek westward across the prairies, plains, and mountains.

Venturing into the Far West in mid-nineteenth century on a trip that would take four or five months necessitated careful foresight and planning. The road to California, however, would not be hard to follow, for thousands of emigrants during earlier years had already beaten down the sod and sagebrush, and only a blind man would have been unable to follow it. But there remained the more difficult matter of choosing supplies and equipment. Emigrants for the most part were greenhorns ignorant of the needs of the trail and the demands it would make upon them. Should they use mules, horses, or oxen? What foods and medicines should they carry and how much? What kinds of clothing were best (some women introduced bloomers, and lucky persons had goggles to keep irritating dust from their eyes)? How much should they take in the way of utensils, tools, furniture, bedding, and a hundred other items? Most took too much, and the road became strewn with discarded belongings — a junkyard stretching halfway across the country.

Travelers like Wayman found answers to many of their questions in guidebooks and from conversations with outfitters. Guidebooks, which cost about twenty-five cents apiece, were plentiful and ranged from the worthless to the adequate. Emigrants relied upon them for a knowledge of distances, camping places with good water, grazing areas for their cattle, sites where wood was available, and the like. Sometimes the information they contained was completely worthless. But internal evidence in Wayman's diary shows that he had the newest and one of the best: *The Travelers' Guide Across the Plains upon the Overland Route to California,* by P. L. Platt and N. Slater, published in Chicago in 1852.[27] If he read the "General Directions" in this little book, he found useful condensed information — less than some other guidebooks offered but much that was sound enough. Platt and Slater, unlike some authors, had been over the trail and wrote from personal knowledge of its conditions. They recommended oxen over horses or mules and suggested four or five yoke for each wagon. Since Wayman's group took only one light wagon, they needed fewer animals (Wayman's share of the cost of the oxen was $70.00). "Your wagons," Platt and Slater recommended, "should not be very heavy, but well made; and should have two good lock chains — one on each side" (p. xvii). In time Wayman and his friends found this piece of advice very sound.

Their choice of food depended largely upon what would keep well. If the Wayman party heeded Platt and Slater, they took ". . . flour, corn-meal, (kiln-dried), hard-bread, crackers of different kinds, side bacon and hams, tea, coffee, sugar, different kinds of dried fruits, beans and rice; to which may be added, some pickles, a little vinegar, and some good butter, well worked and well packed,

---

[27] A copy of the original edition is extremely scarce. A modern reprint has been published by John Howell (San Francisco, 1963); all citations are to this edition.

and stowed in the bottom of the wagon" (p. xvii).[28] Their diet was supplemented from time to time with fresh fish, antelope, and buffalo. Each man, Platt and Slater believed, should carry a minimum of 300 pounds of provisions. Adequate clothing and bedding as well as a gun apiece were also essentials. One recommendation Wayman's group largely ignored: "Along the worst parts of the route," Platt and Slater advised, "companies ought to consist of not less than twenty-five men. That number, by faithful guarding can come [through] safely. In the midst of the emigration a smaller number might get through without trouble" (p. xviii). It is worth noting that Wayman's party had no trouble at any time with shortages of food nor serious difficulty with Indians. In fact, their entire journey was notably free of emergencies. They did not press their animals hard, rested them when necessary, and in general managed the whole trip with good sense.

Because their route is described in detail in the text of Wayman's diary and in the footnotes, only its general outlines might be given here.

From St. Joseph they went nearly due west, struck the Big Blue and Little Blue rivers south of today's Marysville, Kansas, and then headed northwest up the Little Blue toward the Platte, which they followed to the confluence of its main branches. Here they shifted over to the North Platte, and along its dreary stretches passed such landmarks as Courthouse and Jail Rocks, Chimney Rock, and Scotts Bluff, and finally came to Fort Laramie. After a layover near the fort, they set out once again along the North Platte, leaving it eventually (west of modern Casper, Wyoming) for the Sweetwater, which took them directly to South Pass. Crossing the Continental Divide here, they soon hit Pacific Creek and followed it to the Big Sandy. Down the Sandy they went as far as Kinney's cutoff[29] and then traveled west across the Green River and eventually to Hams Fork. Making their way through the mountains lying to the west, they struck Bear River and followed it north to where Soda Springs, Idaho, is now located.

West of here they had a choice to make, and they apparently made it upon the recommendation of Platt and Slater. They could either take the road that went northwesterly to Fort Hall and the Snake River or follow the Hudspeth cutoff, which went almost due west to the Raft River, where the cutoff joined the road coming diagonally down from Fort Hall. They chose the Hudspeth

---

[28] A list of expenses in the diary shows that Wayman took the following items with him or bought them along the way: one-half pound citric acid, an ax, whisky, a kettle, a coffee pot, hams, salt, buffalo robes, a lariat, fifty pounds of flour, lead, several pairs of moccasins, horse shoe nails, a bushel of potatoes, corn meal, meat, pies, hay, and shirts.

Alpheus Graham, another 1852 emigrant, lists in detail the supplies he took: flour, sugar, brandy, nails, tea, coffee, rope, powder, shot, thread, cheese, tartaric acid, kettles, pins, liniment, calomel, ginger, ammonia, crackers (125 pounds), dried apples, lemon syrup, jugs, buckets, lead, tar, turpentine, beans, kegs, ink, quinine, castor oil, camphor, sulphur, bacon, vinegar, soap, molasses, salt, caps, needles, beads, soda, rice, a demijohn, cayenne pepper, sweet oil, peppermint, and opium ("Journal," p. 20).

[29] See diary for June 26, 1852, and note 39.

# INTRODUCTION

route, although it saved little distance or time. It was a good enough road to follow in 1852, having been in constant use during the summer months since 1849.

As did hundreds and perhaps thousands of other emigrants, Wayman and his party plodded through the mountains of Idaho to the City of Rocks, through the Goose Creek Mountains to Thousands Springs Valley, and eventually came out upon the Humboldt River. They followed this river through some of the most barren country of the entire trip, but it was comparatively free of serious obstacles. By now, though the animals of many travelers were beginning to give out, and Wayman passed hundreds of dead or dying animals and abandoned wagons. The Humboldt curved south to the Carson River, which led them finally to the great barrier stretching across their path — the towering Sierra Nevada Mountains. Up its sheer slopes they struggled at last over Carson Pass, the most difficult stretch of the entire trip. Once across the summit, Wayman and his companions soon arrived at Placerville, where the party broke up, each man now going his own way.

### IV.

IT HAD BEEN A JOURNEY which no one today could possibly experience except vicariously in the written accounts of the emigrants themselves. These show us what men, women, and children endured. In their accounts we see suffering, despair, and defeat; strength and weakness; knowledge and ignorance. We watch some traveling with wagons and teams, some pushing wheelbarrows, and others walking with their provisions on their backs. Ambition and thwarted hope, love and hatred, determination and discouragement, birth and sudden death traveled side by side. Wayman saw it all.

Enormous numbers of people crowded the road to Oregon and California during 1852. As the trails from Independence and St. Joseph converged, the line of traffic was literally endless. "As far as the eye can reach to the east and to the west," Richard O. Hickman observed, "nothing is to be seen but large trains of wagons and stock. When I beheld it first I could not help asking myself where all this mass of human beings came from. . . ."[30] The dust they stirred up was so heavy that sometimes he could hardly see his teams ahead of him. Ezra Meeker, who was also part of the 1852 migration, judged that there was an almost unbroken line of emigrants and animals extending over five hundred miles. On May 28 at Fort Kearney, Alpheus Graham, another of these 1852 venturers, reported 3,280 teams on the south side of the Platte and about 1,000 on the north with little grass to feed them.[31] Sometimes three and four wagons

---

[30] Hickman, *Overland Journey to California in 1852*, p. 5.

[31] Meeker, *The Ox Team*, pp. 38–39, and Graham, "Journal," p. 7. Available statistics concerning the migration are often impressive. The *Sacramento Daily Union* on August 17, 1852, published the results of a dispatch from the St. Louis *Republican*, which reported that between May 29 and June 11 the following had passed Fort Kearney: 16,362 men; 3,242 women; 4,666 children; 5,325 wagons; 6,538 horses; 4,606 mules; 1 hog; 59,392 cattle; 10,523 sheep; 100 to 150 turkeys; 4 ducks; and 3 guinea hens.

moved side by side with no possibility for anyone to pass. One traveler expressed the opinion that where he was at one point, 15,000 wagons were still behind him. He could see neither the beginning nor the rear of the line, so far did it extend in both directions.

Such great numbers of people included all strata of society. A. M. Crane, another one of this great mass of people on the move that year, found that the majority were of the lowest sort, ". . . among whom the most horrid profanity and degrading vulgarity and obscenity of language is nearly universal. Their blaspheming is generally vented upon their oxen, and is of a character too horrid to defile my paper with." In contrast, he said, were respectable people "who entirely eschew all these vices. Sometimes one meets here a gentleman or lady of refinement and education but not often."[32] Many travelers, he was surprised to find, were families, some with six to twenty-four children apiece. "One wagon in particular struck my fancy[,] being occupied wholly by the ladies and children. . . . Good easy seats — side curtains to roll up &c. The cry of a young babe seemed so domestic that it almost made me homesick."[33]

Such vast numbers of animals and human beings passing over much the same road and camping at the same camp grounds without sanitation made defilement of water and soil inevitable. Flies spread disease-bearing filth. Deadly illnesses, especially cholera, became unavoidable and so commonplace that every 1852 diary is filled with mention of death and graves. This is such a prevailing theme that I can give only a slight indication of its magnitude. It is this aspect of the migration, with its great toll in human lives, that is most appalling.

Although many wagons carried supplies of medications, the emigrants were hardly capable of diagnosing their ailments accurately or prescribing for them effectively; and even doctors, when they could be found, were little better able to treat dread diseases like cholera with the medicines at hand.[34] Some emigrants

---

[32] "Journal," p. 22.

[33] *Ibid.*, p. 17a.

[34] For various studies of disease on the trail, see John E. Bauer, "The Health Factor in the Gold Rush Era," in *Rushing for Gold*, John W. Caughey, ed., pp. 97–108; Georgia W. Read, "Diseases, Drugs, and Doctors on the Oregon-California Trail in the Gold-Rush Years," *Missouri Historical Review*, XXXVIII, 260–76; Groh, *Gold Fever*, Chapters 3 and 9; and Dunlop, *Doctors of the American Frontier*. Dunlop refers to a physician who went to Oregon in 1850 who estimated that between two and three thousand persons bound for Oregon died of cholera alone. He treated not less than 700 persons (p. 100). Dunlop also says that Dr. John Powell sometimes went fifty miles to deliver babies to emigrant mothers and to treat people suffering from typhoid fever and cholera. Dr. Powell's experience led him to believe that contaminated water was the main cause of such illnesses, and he urged efforts to keep water pure (*loc. cit.*).

## INTRODUCTION

even tried to overcome the effects of bad water by adding whiskey in hopes of purifying it.[35]

With such inadequate efforts to stem the spread of cholera, it is no wonder that the disease hit many people. Meeker found "The scourge of cholera on the Platte in 1852 [to be] far beyond [his] power of description," and he reports the experience of one woman who testified that during the course of two nights and a day, forty individuals in her train died. An entire family of seven succumbed and were buried in a common grave.[36] It was not uncommon for an individual to be well in the morning and dead by evening. One diarist, Jared Fox, recorded a case of sudden death of this kind: "7 o'clock and near sundown," he wrote, "the comrades of [a] dead man are digging his grave and burying him near the road some 10 rods in front of our tent. Looks solemn. . . . Had a brother with him and a wife and children. . . . I have since learned that the brother that was well when he was buried died before morning and was buried after we left that morning."[37]

When Alpheus Graham became ill on June 3, he wrote in his diary: "Very unwell, have the diareaha [sic] bad, had a doctor in this eve, his medicine helped my bowels, but I have a high fever. The boys . . . are all more or less alarmed. The cholera raging all around us."[38] He gradually recovered, but others were not always that fortunate. Some became so discouraged by the threatening disease that they turned back rather than to continue facing the risk.

J. M. Verdenal tells of an instance of this kind. On May 29, 1852, he reported that ". . . during the day we met, [sic] one wagon returning from its intended voyage viz to California; the wagon consisted of two men, both brothers one of whom lost his wife ahead leaving him & his brother to take care of 6 children, 1 not more than 12 months old. under this burden with the news he had learned he thought the wiser plan was to return, to the states, the news he spoke of was that, a head of us, the Cholera & Smallpox was raging, in unbated fury, and that many of the emigrants were returning."[39] Yet, trusting "in Providence," Verdenal and his company pushed on. Some tried various expedients other than trusting in Providence to avoid contagion. Alpheus Graham's party, for example, decided to travel at night in an attempt to pull beyond emigrants ahead of them and thus evade the threat of contagion.

Every instance of death on the trail was a cause of heartache, and sometimes the fear of death and the need to hurry on caused a wagon company to ignore the needs of the sick or even to abandon members who were dying. In one such instance a woman and her children stood weeping around the new grave of the husband and father after her company drove away. Nor was it unknown for

---

[35] Crane, "Journal," p. 11.
[36] *The Ox Team,* pp. 80–81.
[37] "Memorandum," p. 12.
[38] "Journal," p. 8.
[39] "Journal," p. 10.

children to become orphans through the deaths of their parents. Margaret Inman tells of carrying ". . . a little motherless babe five hundred miles, whose mother had died, and when we would camp I would go from camp to camp in search of some good, kind, motherly woman to let it nurse and no one ever refused when I presented it to them."[40]

In another instance, a man who had gone to California ahead of his family started back to meet his wife and children, now traveling west to rejoin him. At the meadows on Carson River, he was reunited with his wife at 3:00 o'clock one afternoon but found her dying. Though unable to speak, she recognized him: "she put her arms around his neck and smiled, at 8 o'clock she died leaving three children she had brought with her, the eldest not yet four years old and she but 23. . . ."[41] Such experiences illustrate the anguish of many individuals who started out confident of reaching their hoped-for goals but unaware of the possible hazards in store for them.

It was in the midst of such human suffering that Wayman also traveled. Not infrequently he would be called upon to tend the sick. On the basis of his experience, he reached certain conclusions about disease and its causes on the trail. Writing in his diary on June 30, he made the following observations:

> From the commencement of our journey, the diseases were Diarrhea in two forms, the pale free watery discharges and the Bilious[.] This will be sufficient as a discription, until we left Fort Laramie after which Dyesentery [sic] seemed to take the place of Diarrhea — After reaching the South Pass, we encountered some fever of a Bilious Remittent [?] character, not maligna[n]t, being easily controled, when not associated with disease of the Bowels. I have heard of some deaths occuring from this mountain fever, in such cases I think from what I have seen, that it is the result of bad management, and when death does occur, the immediate cause is Peritoneal inflamation. I have visited some cases & indeed the only serious ones were of this character, This induces me to think that all fatal cases terminate in this way. Peritoneal inflamation seems to be a natural concomitant of this Mountain fever. I have seen a number of cases and all seeme to weare [sic] this tendency. Though if properly managed there is no danger.

Since Wayman and his company went through without any illness, they were probably careful to "manage properly."

But death was not always the result of mismanagement or disease. Sometimes it was the consequence of violence in a wilderness far beyond the reaches of the law where crime occasionally went unpunished and where even murder could take place without reprisal. Alpheus Graham's company, for example, found a dead man floating down the North Platte somewhere beyond Fort Laramie. They brought the body ashore and determined that the man had been killed and

---

[40] "My Arrival in Washington in 1852," *Washington Historical Quarterly*, XVIII, 254.
[41] H. S. Anable, "Journal," pp. 61–62.

# INTRODUCTION

probably tossed into the river.[42] But not all criminal acts went unpunished. Emigrants sometimes took the law into their own hands and dealt severely with persons found guilty of murder.

A good example of punishment which was nearly as brutal as the crime appears in the journal of John Verdenal:

> during the day [Monday, July 5] saw the grave of 7. Miller died June 10th 1852 he was murdered in cold blood by a man named Lafayette Tate.... [The next day] started early crossed Bosame Creek [?] where I gleaned the following particulars of the murdered Tate. It appeared that Tate had informed some one in Miller's train that as soon as he would be out of the reach of Fort Laramie he would kill miller and he (miller) going on one day ahead of the train Tate stabbed him to the heart. Tate was immediately brought before a tribunal of representatives from 200 wagons in the neighborhood. Tate had a fair and impartial trial. by them he was sentenced to be hung and his remains buried but 1 foot below the sod so that his Body should become the prey of the wolves & other animals[.] This sentence was fully carried into effect and thus Tate paid the deep penalty for his crime, when we passed near this day we noticed his grave from which one of his bones protruded forth and his hair was strewed around the grave. It was a shoking sight[.][43]

Then there was also the murder of Mathias Beal (or Beel) by his partner Leo Balsey, which George Stewart calls "... the classical story of wagon-train justice." The shooting, which occurred somewhere between Green River and Hams Fork, is reported in many diaries. On July 3 Alpheus Graham came to the spot where Beal had been murdered. He wrote briefly in his diary: "We passed the grave of Mathias Beal of Boon County, Ky., who had been shot on the 12th day of June by Leon Bolsey of the same place." The next day Graham neared Hams Fork; and "Here," he says, "we saw the grave of Bolsley [*sic*] shot on the 14th of June for the murder of Beal, we have heard particulars."[44]

Stewart has pieced out the affair with many more details. After Balsey was taken into custody, he was tried before a twelve-man jury. Balsey denied none of the testimony, was found guilty, and condemned to be executed by a firing squad at six o'clock the next morning. Six rifles were loaded only with powder, six others with powder and ball. With his back toward the firing squad and kneeling on a blanket, Balsey himself gave the signal to fire. He was buried alongside the trail.[45]

---

[42] Alpheus Graham, "Journal," pp. 10–11.

[43] "Journal," p. 22. Caroline Richardson devoted three pages of her "Journal and Commonplace Book" to recounting this affair; see pp. 63–66.

[44] "Journal," p. 13.

[45] For Stewart's account, see his *The California Trail*, pp. 308–309.

The experiences of the emigrants were not all concerned with grim death and violence, however. There was also entertainment in the camps at night, with singing, dancing, and merrymaking. One John H. Clark, tells of ". . . many musicians belonging to the different encampments surrounding us, and after supper all commenced to practice the sweet tunes that were to enliven us while sitting around the camp fire on the far off plain."[46] Another diarist mentions dancing to the "inspiring strains of the violin" and also of seeing two girls playing an accordion and a guitar as they drove along in their wagon.[47] But diaries report far fewer experiences like these than they do the humdrum details of travel and the numbers of miles covered per day.

Wayman himself especially liked to wander from the road, observing rock formations and classifying specimens which he picked up. His daily entries comment upon familiar landmarks, the annoyance of insects, the monotony of traveling along the Platte, the food he and his friends ate, what they did while resting, the sublimity of the landscape, the weather, and other common details. His diary is relatively free of the sensational aspects that some travelers knew. Like those of most emigrants, Wayman's diary is basically an account of the day-to-day effort to make a few more miles toward the beckoning gold fields. When he reached Placerville, tired of the trip and of the irritating delays imposed by his partners, he felt a profound satisfaction that the long trek was over and that he could now devote his time to the purpose for which he had come. "Well[,] this Hangtown [Placerville] is one of the towns what is a town," he exclaimed in his diary on August 27. "We sold out our interest in all Cattle and a glad[d]er boy never presented himself in this region[.]" He was now ready to visit the gold camps and learn what opportunities they might hold for him.

### V.

RATHER THAN REMAINING in Placerville, Wayman determined to start immediately for the southern mines near Sonora, where his brother James had been early in 1850. He remained in Placerville only from August 27 until the morning of August 29 and then left by stage for Sacramento. On August 31 he took a stage to Stockton, where he arrived the same day, and then went to Sonora on September 1.

Sonora put him close to such mining camps as Columbia, Shaw's Flat, Springfield, and Jamestown, and he spent several weeks moving from one to another looking for a favorable mining opportunity. He wrote in his diary on September 23: "I again, in company with Mr. Cooper and Dr. Butler, tramped among the mountains till noon to day; during which time we passed several mining locations some of which, looked very favorable according to my judgment of such

---
[46] "Overland to the Gold Fields," p. 233.
[47] E. W. Conyers, "Diary," *Transactions of the Thirty-Third Annual Reunion of the Oregon Pioneer Association*, pp. 434–35.

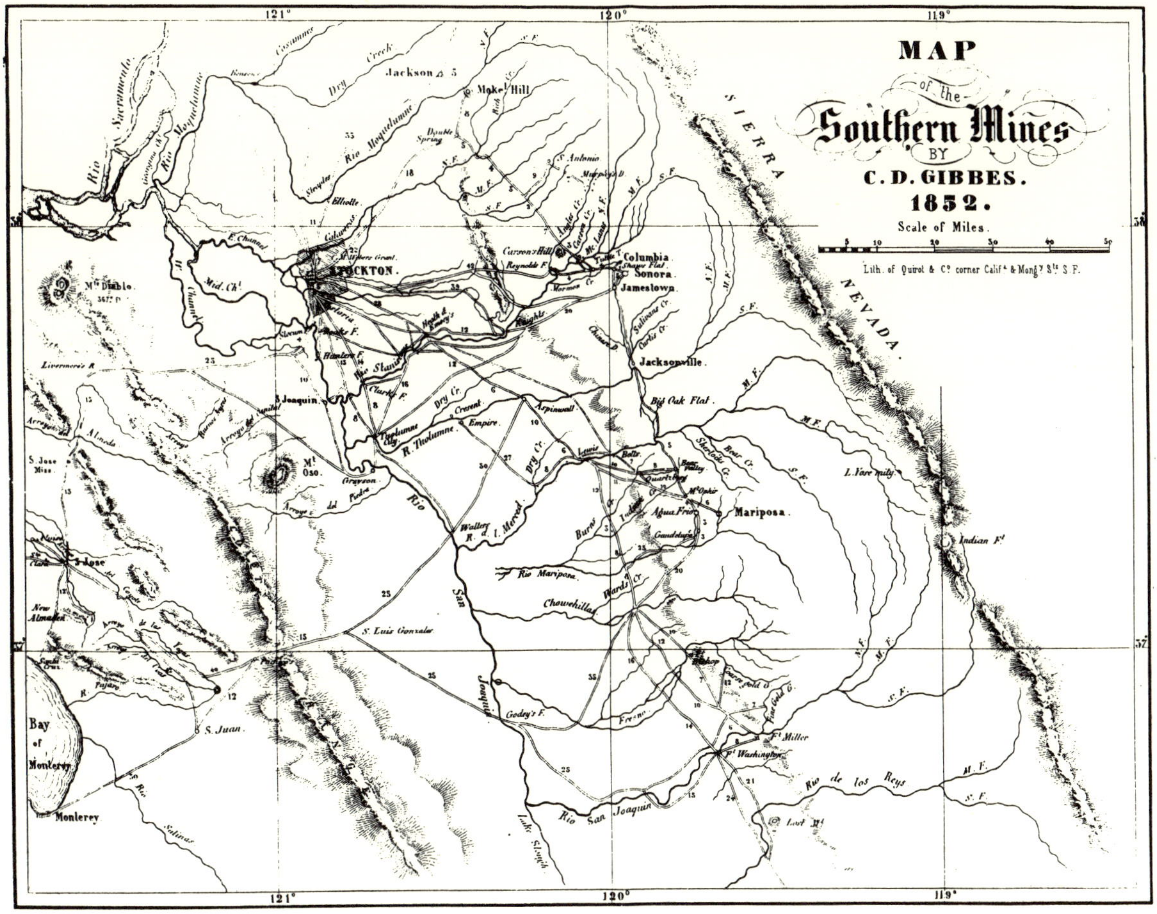
MAP
of the
Southern Mines
BY
C. D. GIBBES.
1852.
Scale of Miles.
Lith. of Quirot & Co. corner Calif. & Mong. Sts. S.F.
SIERRA
NEVADA.
STOCKTON.
Columbia
Sonora.
Jamestown.
Jacksonville.
Big Oak Flat.
Mariposa.
Moke Hill
Jackson
Mt. Diablo.
Mt. Oso.
S. Jose
S. Juan.
Monterey
Bay of Monterey
Rio San Joaquin
Rio de los Reys
R. Tuolumne
Rio Mariposa
Chowchillas
Ft. Miller
Ft. Washington
Indian Ft.
121°
120°
119°

things. I am unimployed as to actual work, Yet I think that I will soon be situated among the Dirt, water, mud and I hope Gold —" On September 30 he was still looking: "I have visited quite a number of mining locations, to see how times are working in this important calling, as I hope soon to be a member of that honorable portion of [the] Community." Yet, by October 1 he still had not found what he wanted, nor had he by October 4.

Then abruptly with October 6, the diary becomes exceedingly sparse, and one can assume that about this time he and his friends had located a claim. The first positive indication is the entry for October 13, in which Wayman wrote only the three words "Worked a little." On October 14 he stated: "Mined all day." From then on, since most of his diary entries consist merely of dates without any indication of his daily activities, it is apparent that Wayman and his associates were busy mining "among the dirt, water, [and] mud." Whether they had struck gold is conjectural, although rival miners may have thought they had. On November 12 their claim was disputed, for on that day Wayman wrote: "Today visit[ed] by a delegation from Sonora, dispossessed us." Nothing further appears concerning this matter, and the diary is silent about Wayman's precise activities during the remainder of the month.

Yet he obviously intended to remain in the area during the winter, for on December 3 he wrote that he "scored timber to day for house." His mining operations must also have continued; on December 9 he stated in his diary: "Our claim changed hand[s] again to day, but changed back immediately." The last diary entry is for March 25, 1853; unfortunately, between December 4 and March 25 Wayman merely jotted down weather conditions or wrote nothing at all except dates. As a consequence, it is impossible to follow his day-by-day activities during this period.

The abrupt break in the diary after March 25, 1853, strongly suggests that Wayman left the mines at this time to visit his family in Indiana. That he actually made such a visit is evident in a letter he wrote to his brother James on February 12, 1854, after he returned to California. Apparently Wayman left there in the spring of 1853, remained in Indiana during the summer and winter of 1853–54, and then started back to California in the spring. This time he traveled by way of Panama, stayed awhile at Acapulco, Mexico, and then took a steamer for San Francisco, where he arrived on April 14.

By now he had put aside the thought of doing any mining himself. His best opportunity, he had decided, was to settle as a physician in a prosperous town and invest his income in mines. The town he chose was Forest City, ". . . situated," he wrote his brother on June 12, 1854, "about 60 miles north of Marysville between the north and middle Yubas." Here, he went on to say, "I have recently bought an interest in a mining claim, which I *think* will pay something very handsome — I Can make at the practice, at least enough to keep myself and hire a hand to work. This is the condition that I have been seeking since my arrival in California. It now remains for time to tell the story — I am in the richest mining district in California. . . ."

18

# INTRODUCTION

He was still in Forest City the next year and using his income to promote his mining investments. Writing to his brother on April 25, 1855, he explained: "I have control of some mining Claims, upon which I have hands at work, and from which I confidently hope to realize my share within 12 months. I can do a business amounting to at least 8000$ in a year, but probably could not collect more than half, if that. There are so many destitute Creatures that you Can't make it Come out right.... So matters wag on here.... From my business I manage to get enough to live *well* and Keep up my mining interests, which is no small item in the way of expences."

His last letter from Forest City, dated August 2, 1858, indicates that he intended to leave there in the following spring and move to San Francisco. Forest City and the surrounding mines were on a decline, owing very largely to new strikes on the Frazer River in Canada, which drew away many California miners. Some of Wayman's patients left without paying their bills, and he seems to have lost heavily as a result. In the meantime a fire had razed the town, and rather than building a new office, Wayman simply rented space for the intermediate period.

He seems not to have carried out his intention of moving to San Francisco, however. With the discovery in 1858–59 of the rich ore deposits in the Comstock Lode in Nevada, a further outflow of California miners took place. Wayman followed and in partnership with Dr. A. W. Tjader[48] set up a new practice in Carson City, Nevada, a community which had been nonexistent when he had crossed the site as an emigrant in 1852. A letter to his brother James which Wayman wrote from here on March 25, 1862, suggests that he may have moved to Carson City during the previous winter: "I am in the practice here — plenty to do, but small returns. Times are, and have been during the past winter, very hard — We hope soon to have easy times in money matters.... This is evidently the richest portion of God's earth, or will be, when fully developed." The letter concludes with the postscript: "I am half promised to marry next fall, but have not fully made up my mind yet. If I do, it will be Kentuck-stock of the Trumbo tribe. You may know them."

The marriage took place not in the fall of 1862 but on February 4, 1863, in Carson City. The bride was Margaret A. Ormsby, and officiating at the ceremony was Orion Clemens, brother of Mark Twain and Acting Governor of Nevada Territory at the time.[49] Margaret Ormsby was a resident of Carson City[50] and the widow of Major William M. Ormsby, who had been killed in a skirmish with Piute

---

[48] See J. Wells Kelly, *First Directory of Nevada Territory* (1862), pp. 89, 91. The following statement appears on p. 91: "WAYMAN & TJADER, physicians, office at Muncton & Warner's."

[49] Witnesses were Dr. A. W. Tjader, Wayman's partner; Lucy Tjader, John J. Musser, Fannie Musser, H. Murphy, P. H. Breyfogle, and Mary Ellen Clemens, wife of Orion. Information about the marriage appears on a marriage certificate sent me by Verla M. Stinson, Recorder, Ormsby County, Carson City, Nevada.

[50] Kelly's *First Directory of Nevada Territory*, p. 86, states: "Ormsby Mrs. res[ides] W side Carson City."

Indians near Pyramid Lake early in May, 1860.[51] She was born February 4, 1826, as Margaret Trumbo in Sharpsburg, Bath County, Kentucky, and married Ormsby there on July 1, 1844. They had one child, Lizzie Jane, born August 2, 1848, in Westmoreland County, Pennsylvania, where the couple lived until Ormsby, with his wife's brother and two of his own, joined the rush to California in 1849. Margaret remained behind with her daughter but later joined her husband. At the time of her marriage to Wayman, she had been a widow for about three years.

After their marriage the Waymans lived in her home at Third and Minnesota Street.[52] Subsequently they moved to San Francisco, where Wayman probably opened a medical office. Here Mrs. Wayman unfortunately died in childbirth on July 23, 1866, a little over three years after her second marriage. Her body was sent to Sacramento by boat and transported over the Sierras in a carriage drawn by four horses to Carson City, where she was buried after a large funeral. Having settled his wife's estate — for she owned many lots and several homes — Wayman returned to San Francisco and took up residence in a small hotel on Market Street. Here on January 15, 1867, just seven months after his wife's death, he also died. A death notice appeared in the *San Francisco Bulletin* on that day which reads: "In this city, January 15th, Dr. J. H. Wayman, a native of Kentucky, aged 46 years and 5 months."[53]

Burial took place in Carson City on January 20 under the auspices of the Masonic Lodge, of which Wayman had been a charter member,[54] his body being

---

[51] References in the Ormsby family files, Nevada Historical Society, give various dates for his death: May 10, May 12, and May 14. He had come overland to California in 1849. In Sacramemto he operated a mint, subsequently dealt in stocks and real estate, and also operated a stage line between Sacramento and Marysville, California. Later he became a stage agent in Genoa, Utah Territory, and played an important part in the movement to establish Nevada Territory. With Abraham V. Z. Curry (the "Curry — *Old* Curry — Old *Abe* Curry" of Mark Twain's *Roughing It,* Chapter XXV), he laid out Carson City, which became the capital of the territory and of the future state. Here in 1859 he built a hotel, named the Ormsby House, located at the corner of Carson and Second streets. As the leading hotel, it served as a stopping place for the Overland stage; and when Sam Clemens and his brother Orion arrived in 1861, they secured lodging here (Effie Mack, *Mark Twain in Nevada,* pp. 73–74. A photograph of the building faces p. 73). Ormsby County, of which Carson City is also the county seat, is named for Major Ormsby. Some of the above information comes from the files of the Nevada Historical Society.

[52] Information that they lived here in the Ormsby home is from Mrs. Wayman E. Ballenger.

[53] From a photostatic copy made available by the Bancroft Library, University of California at Berkeley. The Virginia City, Nevada, *Territorial Enterprise* published the following notice on January 17, 1867, p. 2: "Dr. J. H. Wayman died in San Francisco. Body shipped to Carson City, Nevada, for burial." I am indebted to Silas E. Ross, Sovereign Grand Inspector General in Nevada, for this item from the *Enterprise.*

20

MARGARET ORMSBY. From a small photograph probably made in Carson City in May, 1860, about three years before her marriage to Dr. Wayman.

interred alongside his wife's. Both were re-interred in 1885 in an Oakland, California, cemetery.[55]

Although Wayman's life was not spectacular and he achieved no position of prominence, he was, nevertheless, a good representative of the class of professional people who joined the great migration to California in the middle of the last century. What makes him especially interesting today is the detailed diary of his overland journey in 1852. As a diary it is better than most, and it enables us over a hundred years later to understand in some measure the life of the westering pioneer and to reflect upon the way in which a pristine wilderness was taken over by a civilized race bent upon exploiting its resources. The diary shows Wayman to have been vigorous and energetic, curious about what he saw

---

[54] Wayman, who had been active in Freemasonry and other fraternal organizations in Forest City and in nearby Downieville, California, was a charter member of the Carson City Masonic Lodge when it was organized on February 13, 1862 (Information from Grover W. Russell, currently the secretary of the Carson City lodge. See also C. W. Torrence, *History of Masonry in Nevada*, pp. 2–4. Silas Ross, cited above, has furnished me with a copy of this citation from Torrence). It is likely that Wayman became acquainted with Mark Twain, who, according to an old visitor's record, visited the lodge on February 27, 1862, and subsequent dates (see Torrence, p. 4). Owing to the fact that Orion Clemens officiated at the marriage of John and Margaret Wayman, it appears more than likely that Wayman may have been well acquainted with both Clemens brothers.

[55] A rather interesting set of circumstances lies in the background of this event. In a letter to his brother James, March 25, 1862, Wayman wrote: "I am pleased to learn, that Willard is making manly strides towards the Completion of his professional studies [medicine]. When he graduates, I would like very well to have him Come to this Country, and do business with me. A fine field is open here, and I can give him plenty to do — What say you?" Willard Gross Wayman, John Wayman's nephew, was the son of James Vallores and Maria Louisa Wayman and had been born in Cambridge City, Indiana, on April 8, 1839. After receiving his medical degree, he accepted his uncle's invitation and joined him in Carson City. Upon the deaths of Margaret and John Wayman, Willard Wayman became Lizzie Jane's guardian and eventually her husband. They lived for a time in Carson City but later resided in San Francisco, where, Mrs. Wayman E. Ballenger informs me, he ". . . gained prominence as head of the Medical Association. . . ." They had two children, Willard Ormsby (b. 1871) and Guy Trumbo (b. 1875). Dr. Willard Wayman died on May 15, 1878, and his widow eventually married Arthur Donnell of Oakland, California. According to the *Reese River Daily Reveille*, May 16, 1885, p. 2, "Mr. Arthur Donnell . . . has been in Carson several days. He is the husband of Lizzie Ormsby, who is better remembered in Carson as formerly the wife of young Dr. W[a]yman. Mr. Donnell, at the wish of his wife, has caused the disinterment of the bodies of Major Ormsby, Mrs. Margaret A. W[a]yman . . . , and of Dr. J. H. W[a]yman, which have for many years lain in the old cemetery at the foot of the hill west of Carson City. The three bodies have been forwarded to Oakland for reburial" (From the files of the Nevada Historical Society).

## INTRODUCTION

along the great highway to the West, honest, helpful to fellow emigrants, sometimes impatient but determined — a part of that pioneer stock which makes up the backbone of western American history. It was these people whom Walt Whitman had in mind when he sang in 1865 of a "resistless restless race":

> We detachments steady throwing,
> Down the edges, through the passes, up the mountains steep,
> Conquering, holding, daring, venturing as we go the unknown ways,
> Pioneers! O pioneers!

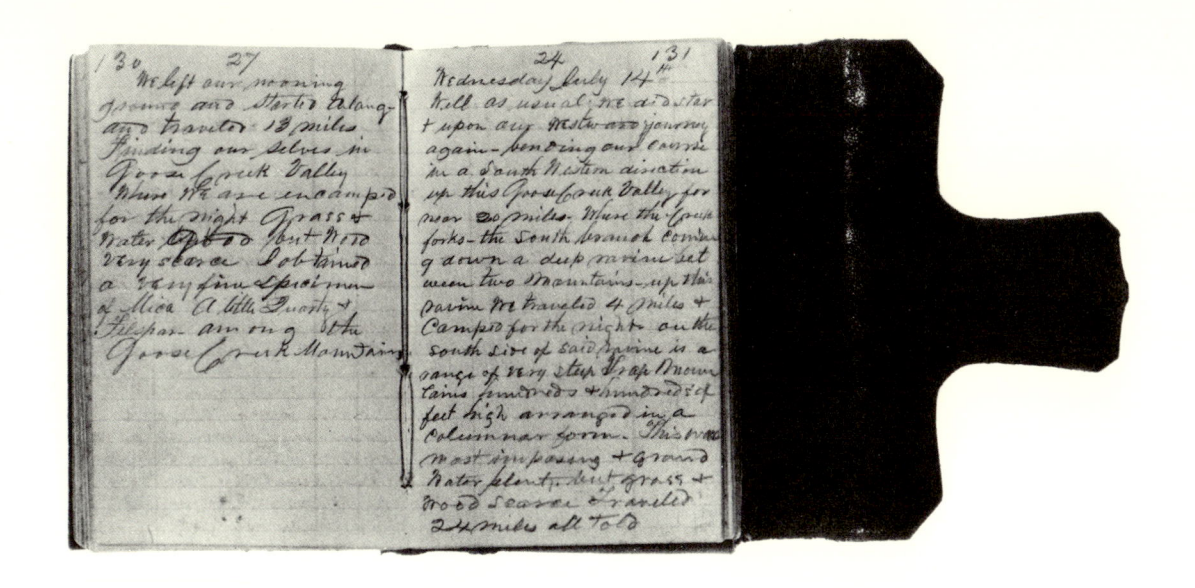

# Diary of Dr. John Hudson Wayman

# March 25 – April 30, 1852

**MARCH 25th 1852**   J. H. Wayman, left Ca[m]bridge city[1] in company with Elbridge Vinton about 9 Oclock in the morning, arrived at Richmond[2] at noon, stoped with D. M. Akin, and remained there till 2 Oclock next morning, left in the stage & went to Hamilton,[3] there boarded the cars & arrived in Cincinnati by noon — Remained in Cinti [*sic*] during[4] the 27. 28. 29 & 30.

[1] Cambridge City, Wayne County, Indiana, is located in the eastern part of the state. Wayman owned a house and lot here.

[2] Richmond, Indiana, about fifteen miles east of Cambridge City, is the seat of Henry County.

[3] Hamilton, Ohio, is thirty-four miles southeast of Richmond and north of Cincinnati on the Miami River.

[4] The numerals 7 and 8 are crossed out following *during*.

**[MARCH 31]**   Wednesday the 31st left on board the Steamer North River bound for St Louis —

**[APRIL 4th]**   Sunday morning the 4 of April, landed at St. Louis —[5] remained there the 4. 5. 6 & Wednesday the 7th left that Port on board the Steamer Clipper No. 2.[6] for St Jo 8. 9. 10.

[5] During April, numerous diarists reported throngs of California-bound emigrants in the streets and docking areas of St. Louis. One of them, Alpheus Richardson from Ohio, observed: "The streets are literally crowded with people and on the wharf there is not room enough for a dray to turn around scarcely for the crowd of people, drays, carriages and wagons bound for California, and provisions which are ready to be shipped" ("Diary," pp. 1–2). Complete bibliographical data for all citations appear in the bibliography.

[6] Although John H. Clark went up the Missouri to St. Joseph on this same steamship later in the month, his observations probably give a good idea of the conditions that Wayman also

witnessed: "Here we began to see the rush for California; a string of adventurers like ourselves came thronging on board until every hole and corner in this spacious ship was full to overflowing. . . ." The next day he wrote: ". . . Still in port and the cry is: 'Still they come.' What are we to do with so many passengers? We were loaded yesterday, but a steamboat, like an omnibus, is never full" ("Overland to the Gold Fields of California in 1852 . . . ," ed. Louis Barry, *Kansas Historical Quarterly*, XI, 230).

[April 11th] Sunday the 11 we arrived at Boonville[7] & remained till morning. this little Boonville is one of the most heartsom places that I ever saw, I like it.

[7] Settled in 1810 as a frontier stockade, Boonville (named for Daniel Boone) is located approximately 150 miles from St. Louis on the south side of the Missouri. When Wayman was there, it was an important trading center for pioneers.

[APRIL] 12 —

[April 13th] Tuesday 13th arrived at Lexington[8] Mo. & visited the remains of the ill fated Saluda.[9]

[8] Lexington is located some forty miles east of Kansas City on the south bank of the Missouri. Its history goes back to 1819. At one time it was the westernmost starting point for the Santa Fe Trail. James A. Pritchard described it in 1849 as being unsurpassed "in beauty or fertility" and heavily timbered (*Overland Diary of James A. Pritchard*, p. 53).

[9] The *Saluda*, a side-wheeled steamer, exploded at Lexinton on April 9, three days before Wayman visited the wreckage. Two hundred persons bound for Salt Lake and California lost their lives, and for several weeks men probed the water for bodies. Most diarists who traveled up the river refer to it. One of them noted that men were ". . . digging from the hulk . . . such articles as were of value, or to ascertain if there were any dead bodies, to give them burial. I suppose they had found many for they had a line on which was hung promiscuously men, women, & children's clothes . . ." (Lodisa Frizzell, *Across the Plains to California in 1852* . . . , p. 8). Another reported that ". . . nothing but the bare hull remained — heavy articles were thrown up nearly half a mile from shore. They said eyes, fingers & toes of the poor unfortunate suffere[r]s were found on the shore & [at] quite a distance" (MS journal of Mary Stuart Bailey, p. 3). John H. Clark stated that "The boat is a total wreck and marks of the terrible catastrophe are still plainly visible on the shore" ("Overland to the Gold Fields," p. 231). See also Phil. E. Chappell, "A History of the Missouri River," *Transactions of the Kansas Historical Society, 1905–1906*, IX, 288, 310.

[APRIL] 14. 15. 16. Stoped at Weston[10] Mo. and on Saturday the 17th in the evening arrived at St. Jo.[11] I and Mc went up in town, & feeling a little hungry stoped in a shanty and called for 2 Oister Soupes; after wating a long hour, our host presented us with 2 shin poultices well done, — Well I was beaten, we laughed at them until we attracted the attention of the whole house, after which, feeling a little asshamed of my rudeness turned about and ate it up like a good boy — Sunday the 18 went into Camp 23 crossed the river and took up our abode amonge the Indians.[12] we remained here during the 24. 25. 26. 27. 28. 29 & 30.

---

[10] Weston lies on the east bank of the Missouri River a short distance north of Fort Leavenworth, Kansas.

[11] Started as a trading post in 1826, St. Joseph, Missouri, by 1852 was an important outfitting center and starting point for emigrants bound for Utah, Oregon, and California. It is located on the east bank of the Missouri River and is the seat of Buchanan County. Estimates by emigrants as to its population in 1852 vary from three to four thousand persons. Henry S. Anable, who passed through St. Joseph for California in the spring of that year, observed that it was ". . . filled with emigrants to California and Oregon, the hills, valleys, and docks are covered with the tents of the emigrants, Horses, Cattle, mules and every kind of Vehicle crowd the streets, many have already crossed the river and some are far on their way" ("Journal," p. 6). John H. Clark noted that "Oxen, horses and mules are brought in from the surrounding country to sell; the merchant has anticipated all the wants of the emigrant and has everything needful for an 'outfit'" ("Overland to the Gold Fields," p. 232). See also Walker D. Wyman, "The Outfitting Posts," in *Rushing for Gold*, ed. John W. Caughey, pp. 18-21.

[12] Crossing the Missouri created problems for the many emigrants who converged upon St. Joseph. Mrs. Lodisa Frizzell observed in her diary: "Teams [were] crossing the river all the while, but there is not half ferry boats enough here, great delay is the consequence, besides the pushing & crowding, to see who shall get across first. There is every description of teams & waggons; from a hand cart & wheelbarrow, to a fine six horse carriage & buggie; but more than two thirds are oxen & waggons similar to our own; & by the looks of their loads they do not intend to starve" (*Across the Plains to California*, p. 10). John H. Clark said that there were several ferries as well as a steamboat, but emigrants still experienced a delay of two or three days. Rates were one dollar per wagon and fifty cents for each animal ("Overland to the Gold Fields," p. 230).

Once across the Missouri, travelers were in the northeast corner of Kansas. *Travelers' Guide . . . to California*, by P. L. Platt and N. Slater, which Wayman's party appears to have used, states that once across the ferry, ". . . you pass over a heavy-timbered bottom, which in many places is soft and miry, and in wet seasons of the year is exceedingly difficult. This is the heaviest body of timber through which the road runs in passing from the Missouri river to the Nevada mountains" (San Francisco, 1963, p. 1).

# May 1 – May 31, 1852

**[MAY 1st]** On the first day of May, we started on our westward journey — our first days travel found us 22 miles from the Bluffs on Woolf river. Sunday the 2 we crossed Woolf river & camped.[1]

---

[1] This was a small stream with steep banks. Wayman's party probably crossed on a toll bridge constructed by Indians, who charged a toll variously reported as fifty cents or one dollar per wagon. John H. Clark said the bridge was about fifty feet long and that on the day he was there (May 9) "not less than 1,500 wagons" crossed it. The Indians demanded silver coin, not gold ("Overland to the Gold Fields," p. 235). Lydia Rudd said of these Indians: "Some of them [had] on no shirt only a blanket, while others were ornamented in Indian style with their faces painted in spots and stripes feathers and furs on their heads beads on their neck brass rings on their wrists and arms and in their ears armed with rifles and spears" ("Diary of Overland Journey . . . ," no pagination; entry for May 7).

Platt and Slater give the distance from St. Joseph as twenty-seven miles instead of twenty-two (*Travelers' Guide*, p. 1).

**Monday 3rd** we packed up & traveled 14 miles, passing the Mission house —[2]

---

[2] A. M. Crane refers to this institution as "Iowa Mission and farm of about 200 acres sustaind [*sic*] by Methodists." Here his company learned that 700 wagons had already passed ahead of them. See his "Journal of a Trip Across the Plains in 1852," pp. 1a and 3. Other diarists also refer to the mission, which Platt and Slater placed four miles west of Wolf River. Esther Hanna placed the mission thirty-one miles west of St. Joseph (Eleanor Allen, *Canvas Caravans*, p. 25).

**Tuesday 4.** The company went on, and I and Mc returned to the Mission house for the purpose of buying a yoke of oxen: failing there, we went on and crossed the river at Iowa Point 6 miles further. We traveled 5 miles in the country to Oregon town,[3] left there and lodged with a Mr Baldwin[.] Wednesday 5 we visited Mr Hawn of whom we baught a yoke of Oxen and pushed for the ferry. arrived there about 8 Oclock. A drove of cattle was being ferried over, and we

MAY 1 - MAY 31, 1852

were forced to wate. During our stay there we visited Negro Peter, of whom we baught some whiskey and grub, and became acquainted with Indian Mary, we made a bargain with Mary for some cat meat, and just as we were ready to fill our part of the contract a company of d—d Indians passed along and spoiled our fun.[4] Mary crossed the river with us in the hope that we might come it, but we had not the time to stay. We traveled all day and all night till about day light. it rained like Hell all night. *very cold.*

[3] Unidentified. Probably a camp site for Oregon-bound emigrants. Wayman's expense account shows that "near Oregon town" he paid $70 for a yoke of oxen.

[4] "Oh God how rosy" is inserted at this point between lines.

**Thursday 6[th]** Early in the morning we eat grub with a Lady & three gents and pushed on. we caught up with our Company late in the evening.

**[Friday] 7[th]** Made a good drive  Camped on the Nemaha.[5]

[5] On modern maps this appears as the South Fork of the Nemaha River in Nemaha County, Kansas.

**[Saturday] 8[th]** Traveled to and Camped on[6] Stony Creek,[7] and helped to bury a young man after night.

[6] The letters *th* are crossed out following *on*.

[7] "In the bottom of this stream are large stones. The Indians call it Vermillion Creek. From its banks they get red clay with which to paint their faces" (Platt and Slater, p. 2). The Big Vermilion is a tributary of the Big Blue and flows into it from the northeast.

**Sunday the 9th** We arrived at Big Blue river —[8]

[8] Wayman would have read the following passage in Platt and Slater: "This is a fine stream, some four or five rods wide, with a swift current, generally three or four feet deep. Fish are often caught in it. . . . Plenty of wood and grass. . . .

"The latter part of the distance between the Big and Little Blue rivers will be found more hilly than any other part of the route yet passed over. There are numerous steep pitches which will require the use of lock chains.

"About ten miles out from the Big Blue, you pass the intersection of the Independence road with the St. Joseph road" (pp. 2-3).

The crossing of Big Blue, which flows south into the Kansas River, was about eight miles below present-day Marysville, Kansas. Where John H. Clark crossed, there was, he wrote, ". . . a private postoffice, a dramshop, hotel and a ferry, the business all under one roof" ("Overland to California," p. 237). Letters cost a dollar to mail; a dram of whisky was seventy-five cents, and a meal one dollar and a half. Ferriage per wagon was an exhorbitant four dollars.

31

**[Monday] 10th**  we crossed the river and Camped on the west side. One of our party set his hook and caught a Catfish weighing not less than 12 lbs. We had a fine mess of fresh fish.[9] In the afternoon of this day it rained, Oh Hell how it rained.[10]

---

[9] Note that Wayman's companion followed Platt and Slater's suggestion about catching fish.

[10] Other diarists also mention this torrential downpour of May 10: ". . . I noticed a storm was approaching from the west," wrote Richard O. Hickman, "and by the time we were ready for starting, the rain commenced descending in torrents. Both of the boys crawled into the wagon, and I had to take it. I have seen rain in Illinois, but it was not worth talking about. . . . in less than a half hour I was standing in water over my boot tops. I don't want to be in many rains on the plains" (*An Overland Journey to California in 1852*, p. 4). See also Esther Hanna in Eleanor Allen, *Canvas Caravans*, p. 25.

---

**[Tuesday 11th]**  Tuesday morning the 11th we took our line of march,[11] traveled about 22 miles & camped on Cotton Wood creek[.][12]

---

[11] The folowing interlineation appears at this point: "met Osage Indians on their return from the Pawnee Territory 'war'."

[12] "Good place to camp" (Platt and Slater, p. 3).

---

**Wednesday 12th**  we journied 22½ miles & camped on Little Sandy[.]

**Thursday 13th**  made a drive of 24 miles, and Camped on Ale-Nease Creek[.][13]

---

[13] Ale Neas' Creek in Platt and Slater, p. 3.

---

**Friday 14th**  made a short drive of 10 miles, arrived at Little Blue.[14] suned and aired our provisions, caught some fish, made a pot of bean soupe, lived fine[.]

---

[14] A. M. Crane wrote of the Little Blue: "It has high banks, a very swift current, and is from 5 to 8 rods wide and 3 to 6 feet deep. The water has a dark turbid appearance but is good drinking water and becomes clear by stirring in a little meal and settling it" ("Journal," p. 74). See also Platt and Slater, p. 3. The Little Blue flows into the Big Blue below Marysville, Kansas.

---

**Saturday 15th**  Remained in Camp to day until noon, made a good half days drive & Camped in a Burr oak bottom. I stood sentinel & found it very cold & windy.

**Sunday 16th**  This was an awful cold & windy day — the most disagreeable, outrageous day that I ever experienced[.] Were it not Sunday I would not take

# MAY 1 - MAY 31, 1852

any account of it. The road since we struck the Little Blue River is and has been much better, being more level. The scenery is some changed[.]

**Monday 17th 1852** Got an early start, left the Little Blue, and bore to the right, in the direction of the Platt —[15] Took dinner on a high level plane saw four Antelope; the boys give them a hard chase, but could not get near enough to Kill any — Last night was awful cold, some ice, & a very heavy frost this morning —[16] Encamped on a level plain; saw several Antelope in the afternoon, but Killed none. Since we struck the Little Blue, the scene has been changed, the country being more level & easy[.] From the Bluffs at St Jo, it has been one continued sea of Prairie, without any material change. The streams are generally narrow deep & crooked with muddy abrupt banks & sometimes quite difficult to cross. The streams & branches are skirted with Cotton Wood, Willow, Elm and shrubby Burr Oak — & this onley occurs along the water courses, I saw pleanty of Wild Rose bushes & Cactus. This continued, unaltered scene, has been presented so long and every day, that it has become tiresome dull & monotonous. The only thing occuring interesting to me in a Geological view, is the continued evidence of Iron, in all & every place, that I have noticed[.] The rock generally are formed of Silica, Horn blend, Carbonate of Lime and Oxide of Iron. Mica & Flint are also common, besides other formations not mentioned. It is now the 17th of May & the grass is too short to do our stock justice. It certainly is a very backward spring[.]

---

[15] That Wayman was relying on Platt and Slater is evident in the following statement in *Travelers' Guide*: "Here, leaving the Little Blue, you bear to the right in a north-westerly direction over high prairie, towards the Platt river" (p. 4).

[16] On this same day A. M. Crane noted: "This morning the wind was blowing a gale from [the] North West, and as cold as Greenland and so continued during the day. I put on three pair pants and 3 woolen shirts besides divers other garments and so made out to keep warm by walking" ("Journal," p. 7b).

**Tuesday MAY 18th 1852** A clear windy day — quite cold. Kept my over coat on all day — saw several Antelope & one Buffaloe cow & calf, killed none. About 5 Oclock P.M. we arrived at the Platt River. This river is about two-hundred yards wide,[17] low banks, & very turbid & muddy[.] Not one stick of timber where we camp — On the north side some woods, more indeed than I have seen since we left the Missouri[.] I saw a Funeral procession by the road side, about 3 Oclock, this looks sad, in this God-forsaken region[.] Grass still scarce.

Indeed we travel no day without seeing a number of old or new graves, with a board of flat stone to mark the last resting place of some unfortunate pilgrim to the land of gold — On the head board, you may see rudely carved by the hand of affection, the Name, Age & Residence of the departed. To me, it looks strange, yes very hard, to know that so many poor fellow Mortals, leave perhaps a good home & come in these Savage wilds to die & be no more only in memory.[18]

As usual we had a Concert last night, by the Woolvs, who seem to be sole proprietors of this prairie during the night time. These concerts are given nightly free gratis, for nothing without any pay, Program or notice. "This is music, what is music."

"The soul that is not moved by concord of sweet sounds is only fit for Strategem, treason and Spoils[.]"[19]

Supper being nearly ready, I will desist from further description, as I feel rather woolfish myself[.] so endeth the 18th day of Old May —

---

[17] The following interlineation appears at this point: "this is only a small arm."

[18] Wayman here touches on an all-too-common experience of emigrants. Silas Miller, in a letter from Oregon to his brother, paraphrases an observer as saying ". . . that from Loup Fork to Ft. Laramie it would average 6 fresh graves to Every mile. From other accounts I should think that this Estimate was none too grate" (MS letter, Nov. 24, 1852, from Salem, Oregon, pp. 7-8).

Jared Fox on May 26 wrote in his diary: "Past one new grave and one not so new and I don't know how many old ones. Saw several by the boards yet standing but I see that graves don't last long here as there is no coffins and many only half buried. They soon fall in and the buffalo and wild animals soon tear and paw them to pieces ("Memorandum," p. 12).

John H. Clark on May 11 witnessed the burial of an only child of an emigrant couple in a cracker box used as a coffin. They piled stones and dirt in the grave and then drove wagons over it. "Perhaps we had cheated the wolf by so doing — perhaps not" ("Overland to the Gold Fields," p. 236). Two days later he passed a grave in which a man had just been buried. Around the spot stood his grieving wife and children, apparently abandoned by their company, which had moved on. "A more desolate looking group," he sadly remarked, "than that mother and her five children presented would be hard to find" (*ibid.*, p. 236). Enoch Conyers reported meeting this woman and her "four or five little helpless children" on July 18 the day before reaching the Bear River; see his "Diary," pp. 466–67. She had bravely continued her journey.

[19] A misquotation of *The Merchant of Venice*, V, i, 83–85: "The man that hath no music in himself, / Nor is not moved with concord of sweet sounds, / Is fit for treasons, stratagems and spoils."

**Wednesday 19th 1852** Nothing unusual to day. saw some Antelope — bad grazing & no wood —[20] Made a moderate drive, & arrived at the long heard of Fort Kearney —[21] No soldiers at home, all having started the day before after a large party of Indians, which had disturbed[22] some emigrants & stole their Mules, killing one of the party — I hope to God, they may find and chastise to [*sic*; the] scoundrels[.] We have as usual to carry wood & water for Camp use, since we struck the Platt river. the road has been level & easy[.]

The Platte river is about one mile in width, on an average; — in some places it is more than 2 miles wide.[23] No wood yet to be found on the south side. We find the river too high to ford, & no ferry boat. We are necessarily forced to keep the south side of the river, for which I am very sorry; yet it may be as well. We can't find wood enough to Kook our grub, "so we have to let the grub be"[.] I am now tired of this interminable prairie, it does me good to see even a respectable bush[.]

Here we are, go it. — *row row*!

---

[20] The following insertion appears between lines: "We met some 30 wagons belonging to the fur company. The teamsters were hard looking nuts."

Several other diarists record meeting these traders. Lodisa Frizzell wrote: "Met a company of fur traders with 16 waggons loaded with buffalo robes, they were very singular in appearance looking like so many huge elephants, & the men, except 2, were half breeds; & indians, & a rougher looking set, I never saw; & their teams which were cattle, looked about used up . . ." (*Across the Plains to California*, p. 17).

John N. Lewis, who also met these men, wrote that there were twenty wagons ("Diary of an Overland Journey to Oregon," p. 36).

[21] Fort Kearney (also Kearny), established in 1848, was situated on the right bank of the Platte River eight miles southeast of present-day Kearney, Nebraska, and 294 miles, according to Platt and Slater, from St. Joseph. Fort Kearney State Historic Park is now located at the site. Numerous emigrant diaries describe the fort as Wayman saw it. One writer observed on May 26 that it ". . . is beautifully situated on the Platte bottom about two miles from the river. It has four or five good-looking frame houses . . . , two or three of them, I should suppose were 50 or 60 feet long. The troops all are decently dressed and the captain appears to be very much of a gentleman" (John Joseph Callison, "Diary," p. 6).

A few days later, another diarist wrote: "I saw any quantity of teams — horses & oxen mules men women & children, all pass through Fort Kerney [*sic*], we left letters there, it is a military post quite a stiring [*sic*] place  the government buildings at least the residents [*sic*] of the officers are very fine  some small framed buildings others built of sods or turf laid up like brick with windows & doors — . . . our people paid 1.00 per pound for horse nails [meat?] Some other things were not so dear but almost everything was so — We went into the register office [and] looked over the names of those who had passed before us some 20,00[0] men and 9,000 women besides cattle & horses mules & sheep to almost any amount, we saw a great many new made graves — there had been a good deal of sickness on the St Joe's road — almost every company had [one word illegible; buried?] one or more . . . ("Journal of Mary Stuart Bailey," p. 6).

An idea of the extent of the migration in which Wayman participated appears in the following figures, which differ from Mary Bailey's given above: 13,089 men; 2,562 women; 3,482 children; 5,482 horses; 3,163 mules; 43,878 oxen; 4,291 wagons; 2,812 sheep; 1 hog (Evan O. Jones, "Overland Diary of a Journey from Wisconsin to California," p. 12). These figures are for only one month. Wayman gives different figures in his entry for May 25.

A. M. Crane stated that the personnel of the fort were very kind to the emigrants and operated a blacksmith shop free of charge ("Journal," p. 12). There was also a hospital, which treated emigrants (John H. Clark, "Overland to the Gold Fields," p. 243).

See also Lyle E. Mantor, "Fort Kearny and the Westward Movement," *Nebraska History*, XXIX, 175-207 and Francis Paul Prucha, *A Guide to the Military Posts of the United States, 1789–1895* (Madison, 1964).

[22] *And* is crossed out after *disturbed*.

[23] Platt and Slater state that the width of the Platte below the confluence of the two branches averaged about three-fourths of a mile. "It has numerous islands somewhat like an archipellago [*sic*], which are more or less covered with small timber, while the shores of the river are almost entirely destitute of it" (p. 4).

**Thursday MAY 20th 52**   This morning was cold & cloudy.[24] We find the water slightly Alkaline, & in consequence, use river water for cooking & drinking purposes.[25] We now have traveled about 50 miles since we struck the Platte river, & find the road smooth & easy. — Rain commenced falling at noon, & continued during the after noon & night, making it very disagreeable & tiersome. No wood yet. So far as we have journied up this Platt river, the bottom is from 2 to 5 miles wide & almost entirely level; When not raining, the road is good.

[24] There was a frost on the night of May 19/20 (John H. Lewis, "Diary of an Overland Journey to Oregon . . . ," p. 29).

[25] Before using this turbid water, Wayman and his companions must have taken note of the following advice in Platt and Slater: "The water of the Platt is saturated with marl, earthy limestone and sand, and has a turbid appearance. Before being used for drinking or cooking purposes, it should be settled by sprinkling a handful of corn meal slowly into a pailful of the water, and stirring it at the same time. It will shortly become quite clear, palatable and wholesome" (p. 5).

**Friday MAY 21st 52**   This morning is a mere continuation of last evening & night, still raining. We have wisely concluded to remain in Camp to day, & let it rain. From an iland [*sic*] in the river, to which we have access, by wading, we get wood enough to Cook and Keep the fier going. Another fine pot of bean soupe & fresh beef, this is good enough for emigrants[.] We all have fine appetites & enjoy this living to perfection. To set down on a Gloomy, dull, Murkey, cloudy, rainy day like this, and discuss a pot of bean soupe & appertenances there to, with a good appetite, is a privilege too good for common sinners to enjoy. *This is my fate,* & I think that I appreciate it, I *know* that I enjoy it very well at least. The river at this point is one mile & a half wide intersperced with numerous small ilands, on which all the woods we see, mostly grow. I feel more solicitude in relation to our stock, than every thing and all else besides; we are remaining in Camp only for the benefit of our cattle; — and it answers as a day of rest for us poor fellow travelers to the World of Spirits.

**Saturday MAY 22nd 1852**   Made a drive to day of about 20 miles; with the same boundless unaltered view ahead. Not one stick of wood to be seen this side of the river — not even a willow bush, on which we have heretofore often depended. This evening finds us about 55 miles west of Fort Kearney encamped on the south bank of the greate Platte river, where it is near one mile & a half wide. The bottom from the river to the bluffs is near[26] three miles wide, which gradually becomes more elevated from the river to the bluffs, where it terminates abruptly in high mounds, Ridges and Ravines, without one bush or shrub to glad the eye. The prospect looks boundless as the Ocean, & I fancy that the hills in the distance, look like towering Ocean billows. Taken in the whole this looks Grand, Sublime, Magnificent & beautiful — It inspires a feeling of awe & veneration to the "Father of Lights"[.] This, I enjoy, I feel well & even good, while contemplating this scene. We here have the best grazing that I have seen since we have been on the road — & this adds to my good feelings[.] Here we are, row row!!

---

[26] Following *near* Wayman struck out the numeral 3.

**Sunday MAY 23rd 1852** This evening finds us encamped again on the south bank of the Platte, in the edge of a woods that skirts the bank of the river at this point — This is the only good place for wood that I have seen since we left the Little Blue river, & I think that we will make good use of it. To day we traveled about 28 Miles, passing over the same Kind of Country over which we have been traveling for some days. With the exception of higher & more rugged bluffs. Indeed the scenery is very imposing & grand, — it suits me. We passed to day two graves that had been robbed by the woolvs[.] I saw two pieces of scull bone near one of the graves[.] This thing of being disintered by the d—d Woolvs, does not quite suit my ideas of a resurrection, yet it seems that some poor fellows has [sic] been thus served.[27] This is one of the finest days that I ever saw, being clear and cool, though very pleasant. This day reminds [me] of pleasant associations at home at one time, & the next moment finds me contemplating the grand view around me, framing my mind for thinking *good thoughts*[.] Killed a rattle snake four feet long 10 rattles — fine snake this.

---

[27] The prevalence of disease among the emigrants caused many deaths, and graves were common. Survivors often had no choice but to inter bodies without coffins in shallow graves. One of them wrote: "We have no tools nor materials for making a coffin so we had to dig his grave with a vault [sic], then wrap the corpse up in a couple of pair of blankets, then cut wild sage, and place it across to keep the sand from pressing too heavily on it. This done, we erected tomb stones and gave him as decent an interment as we could" (Richard O. Hickman, *An Overland Journey to California in 1852*, p. 11).

**Monday MAY 24th 1852** Encamped on a small branch near half way between the river & bluffs — No Wood, no not one stick & for the first time, we resort to Buffaloe chips for fier[.][28] The bluffs to day presented all Kinds of shapes, Mounds, Cones, peaks Ridges & Ravines, doted [dotted] with clumps of Cedar bushes; This together with the sloping plane & skirted river, was superbly magnefficent [sic]. I rode to the bluffs & assended one of those peaks spoken of. Well, talk of sights, scenes, prospects & vews [sic] as you will or may, this acceeded [exceeded] anything that I ever saw read or heard of, for extent & Grandure. Here I examined the formation of rocks, which are very scarce & found them composed of fine sand & Carbonate of lime, being very easily broken, evidently having been hardened by dessication[.] This beautiful scenery I enjoy finely — This day is one of the finest quality, being clear & pleasant. Made a drive of near 25 miles, tolerably good grazing for our stock, which interests me much as anything else at this time. Tomorrow I think we will cross the south branch of the Platte.

---

[28] Dry buffalo dung took the place of firewood on the treeless plains. John H. Clark wrote: "We had read in 'the books' that people traveling over these plains had 'sometimes to use buffalo chips,' and it took us but a little while to come to that conclusion ourselves. We gathered them by the basketful, by the armful and by the handful, and as they were plentiful I guess we gathered a wagon load, set the heap on fire and cooked our supper. The 'chips' worked like a charm and are really a godsend for the traveler in this part of the country — a staple which would be hard to dispense with. . . . were it not for them I hardly know how the traveler in this part of the country would get along" ("Overland to the Gold Fields," p. 245). When Jared Fox reached the buffalo country, he said that the animals had eaten ". . . the grass down like sheep and in many places it looks like a dairyman's cowyard. Tonight we begin to burn buffalo dung to cook by and it does well. Burns readily" ("Memorandum," p. 12).

So dependent were emigrants upon buffalo chips that sometimes the supply became depleted. E. W. Conyers complained of their scarcity ("Diary," p. 441, 442). See also Charles H. Crawford, *Scenes of Earlier Days in Crossing the Plains to Oregon . . .* , p. 9.

**Tuesday MAY 25th**  A very fine pleasant day, Made a drive of near 25 miles, passing through the same country in appearance that we have been traveling over since we found the Platte Valley — This day about 3 O-clock we came to and crossed the south fork of the Platte, where it is a full half mile wide, & at no place more than 18 inches deep, with very low & even banks, — so much so that we drove in & out of the river without any difficulty —[29] Just above the confluence of the two rivers, a high ridge of bluffs presents to your view, all the varieties that belong to the Hill tribe — We here bore to the right & encamped on the south side of the North fork.[30] Again we resort to Buffaloe chips for cooking purposes, and by the by, they answer a very good purpose — The water all along the Platte vally is Alkline, and in consequence we use river water, for drinking and cooking. Here is a note for the 19th page 15 — This list, we obtained from one of the Officers at the Fort,[31] being the number that had passed up to the time we arrived there. 1182 wagons, 11128 oxen, 3640 men, 509 women, 606 Children, 1440 Horses, 1877 mules, 7 sheep & 6 Wheelbarrows.

---

[29] Wayman and his party evidently crossed the South Fork in the vicinity of its junction with the North Fork near where North Platte, Nebraska, is now located. Platt and Slater write of what they call "the lower crossing": "The fords of this fork are all bad. Sometimes one is best and sometimes another; the force of the swift running water constantly moving the quicksands from one place to another in the bed of the stream. Before attempting to cross with a wagon a person should ride across on horseback, and ascertain the best place to ford" (pp. 5-6).

[30] In doing so, the Wayman party followed the advice of Platt and Slater: "If you cross at

# MAY 1 – MAY 31, 1852

this ford bear immediately to your right and keep along the bottom of the North Fork" (p. 6).
31 Fort Kearney

**Wednesday MAY 26th**  Another very fine pleasant day. Nothing unusual to day, save a quantity of small stone, found in the road for a few miles,— These stone were of a different formation & age from any that I had seen since I left the States, being specimens of Granite, Quartz, Silliceous, Argelaceous & schistose rock. The rock on the Bluffs are the common Calcareous variety, being formed principally of Marl Evidently hardened by desiccation — At noon to day, we found a good spring of cold pure water, this was delicious. We stoped this afternoon about 4 Oclock, (after having traveled about 18 miles,) on the south bank of the river, where we encamped for the Night. Last evening one of our neighbor campers killed a fine Buffaloe cow and was kind enough to present us with a fore quarter; This was a fine treat.— we are now living on good fresh beef. The vally here is fast growing norrow [sic][.] Now in site of us, the bluffs form the river bank & in consequence our road will be more uneaven, We are now enjoying a fine prospect, with not one shrub or bush of any kind in site — row row row!!!

**Thursday MAY 27th**  A clear fine day, & very warm indeed the only right warm day that has been out [?], since we started — This morning we left the river & took to the Bluffs, & after traveling about 15 miles, came to the river again;[32] took dinner (a very good one it was too), and at two Oclock, took up our line of march up [sic], and traveled 5 miles, encamping again on the bank of the celebrated Platte river, where we found good grazing for our stock: Journeying to day full 20 miles. No change in the face of the country. The river here is 1 mile wide.

The bluffs neared the river so closely, in some places this afternoon, that we had barely room to drive, indeed at two points we were in the water's edge, though where we are encamped the bottom is a full mile wide. There is so much sameness in the appearance of the country that we have been traveling over, for the last eight days, (though beautiful and interesting) that I hardly know what else to say. Last evening I & Mc started about sun down, Woolf hunting. We rambled over the bluffs until 10 Oclock, & came in Camp good & tired without any Woolves, bad luck,

32 Wayman's party followed Platt and Slater closely: "Twenty-five miles from the ford the road leaves the river. Ten miles farther on you come to Cedar Bluff. At this point take in wood. After passing Cedar Bluff some distance the road comes again to the river" (p. 6).

**Friday MAY 28th**  A clear fine warm day —
Started very early this morning, making a very good fore noon's drive, say 14 miles, passing along near the bluffs finding them often bedecked with, with

39

[*sic*] rose bushes, current bushes, Cedar bushes Dwarf Cherry bushes, & Grape vines; This looked very fine, being a relief from the Monotonous sameness that we had been accustomed to, since we struck the Platte. During the afternoon we came to and passed *Ash Hollow*.[33] This Hollow takes its name from the quantity of Ash timber growing here. it is about one quarter of a mile in width termin[a]ting on either side with abrupt, precipetous high ledges of rock —[34] These bluffs are bedecked here with numerous Cedar bushes & trees, of all sizes — The bottom being bedecked with Grey Ash, Dwarf Cherry, Current and rose bushes, making the air fragrant with their odor. This is the most beautiful, animating and heartsome place that I have seen here, or else where. I have enjoyed the scenery of to day with a very good appetite — Today's travel finds us about 24 miles from our last Camping ground. We are yet on the bank of the Platte[.]

---

[33] In crossing the South Platte where they did, Wayman and his companions avoided the difficult descent into Ash Hollow, which emigrants who crossed the river farther west, near today's Brule, Nebraska, had to make. The wagon road on the bluffs approaching Ash Hollow is still well preserved.

Wayman read in Platt and Slater the following account of Ash Hollow: "This place is so called on account of the ash timber which grows here. There is also a little cedar. It is one of the most hilly, uneven places found upon the route. There are some fifteen or twenty acres covered with ridges and ravines[,] hills and hollows, of various shapes and dimensions" (p. 6).

With the exception of a two-lane highway running through it and a few farm buildings, Ash Hollow is still little changed from emigrant times. It is located on the south side of the North Platte.

[34] The regular trail, which Wayman's group avoided, descended into Ash Hollow from the southwest corner. So steep was the descent from the ridge that wagons, with their wheels locked, were held back by ropes. "Here we were obliged, from the steepness of the road," wrote Howard Stansbury, "to let the wagons down by ropes . . ." (*An Expedition to the Valley of the Great Salt Lake*, p. 41). This method gave rise to the use of a windlass, and the place came to be known as Windlass Hill. A monument marks the spot today. The several points at which wagons were let down are still plainly visible because of eroded gullies where wagon wheels destroyed the sod. Once down, emigrants found Ash Hollow a good camping ground with a fine spring of fresh water. Alonzo Delano wrote in 1849: "Sheltered from the wind by the high banks, the ravine was warmed by the sun, and the cool shade of the trees, as well as the clear water, was delightfully refreshing" (*Across the Plains and Among the Diggings*, p. 24). Stansbury says there were several springs (p. 41).

**Saturday MAY 29th** A warm fair day.

This morning we concluded to cross the river & commenced the operation at 8 Oclock. We were all safely over by noon.[35] The river here is a full mile wide, and from 1 to 5 feet deep, at the present stage of water. We have been anxious to get on the north side, since we found the river first — this being the first crossable place we avail ourselves of the opportunity, confidently expecting

MAY 1 - MAY 31, 1852

to find better grass, and an easier road, without lengthening our journey. We are remaining in Camp to day, since we crossed the waters, for the purpose of resting our stock, airing our provisions and recruiting our *appetites* — During yesterday and a part of the day before, the road lay over a very sandy plain making it quite heavy wheeling and laborous traveling. This sandy road is another annoyance that we expect to partly avoid by crossing at this point. Some of our party are making a wash day of this, others hunting while some are sleeping or lounging. I feel better satisfied now, that we are on the north side. The advantage it may be to us, yet remains to be tested. *Mesketoes numerous*[.]

---

[35] They crossed from the south to the north side of the North Platte. As Wayman indicates below, hope of finding better grass and a less sandy road motivated the change. Because fewer emigrants used the north side, better forage was available.

**Sunday MAY 30th** Some rain early this morning though by 6 Oclock the sky was nearly clear, and we were on march duty. No change in scenery, the road to day has been less sandy than we found it on the south side, and I *do* hope to find this change continue. We have not been in site of any tree bush or shrub during the whole day's travel. This evening finds us encamped on the north side of the Platte, after journeying 20 miles. We have no wood other than what we carried, and no water but this turbid, nasty filthy Platte water—And Buffaloe chips scarce the Prairie having been recently burned, has consumed all or very nearly all of the dry chips — Notwithstanding all this, we are doing quite as well as could be expected. Numerous Prairie dogs & Gophers[36] to be seen any time that you may desire the sight. We are now about one hundred and 25 miles from Fort Laramie, which point I feel quite anxious to see, and expect in a few days to have my curiosity gratified, if no preventing Providince. Had some beans to day, ate a few and feel very well.

---

[36] *Gophers* appears to be written over *Gofers* or *Goffers*.

**Monday MAY 31st & last.** The same old story as usual. A clear, fine and very warm day. Making in all a drive of 22[37] miles camping on the river bank. No wood and Chips very scarce. One of our party killed a Prairie Dog; being the first one that I saw to handle, it become [*sic*] quite interesting to me (Merely for variety sake) to classify the gentleman. After the examination was over, I refered him together, with the Gopher his next neighbor, to the Rodentia family, and so let it rest. They are very numerous in places, having their Holes and Observatories near to each other, presenting quite a town like appearance.[38] Saw a number of very large grey Woolvs to day, though this common as Cat shit under the stairs, in the States.[39] A beautiful grove of cedar bushes several miles in length on the bluffs, on the opposite side of the river —

During all the after noon, we have been in sight of the Court House,[40] and

I presume that we are yet 40 miles from it. We have pretty good grazing for our stock, this is quite an important article on the bill. so far as tested the grass is much better than on the south side.

---

[37] The numeral *22* is written over *20*.

[38] The animal Wayman describes was either the blacktail prairie dog or the whitetail, but probably the former. See William H. Burt and Richard P. Grossenheider, *A Field Guide to the Mammals,* pp. 97–98.

[39] What Wayman saw was more likely coyotes, which have a grayish coat, rather than gray wolves, which have a different habitat than the area Wayman was in. See *ibid,* pp. 73–76.

[40] Courthouse Rock and nearby Jail Rock are isolated bluffs located south of the North Platte in Morill County, Nebraska. They are a few miles south of Bridgeport. Both formations were famous landmarks on the Oregon-California Trail. See Earl R. Harris, "Courthouse and Jail Rocks, Landmarks on the Oregon Trail," *Nebraska History,* XXXXIII, 29–51.

# June 1 – June 30, 1852

**Tuesday JUNE 1st 1852** A sunny warm dry sandy & dusty very dusty day — Drove all day in sight of the Courthouse and Chimney rocks, the former having some resemblance in shape to a common Courthouse.[1] This rock is said to be ten miles from the river, yet it looks incredible that it should be more than three or four miles. The Chimney rock is about 12 miles above the Courthouse, & six miles from the river, it is a high mound of rock for probably two thirds of its hight, then contracting its self into a long shaft, standing purpendicularly[,] reminding one of a spacious dome and spire.[2] In the neighborhood of this rock, are numerous others presenting all shapes and varieties of buildings — I fancy, that this place beares a strong resemblance to an old delapidated, Ancient city, with its rude fortifications, Massive citadels & Mansions in ruins — Since noon to day we have been in sight of Scotts blluff [*sic*] they look grand in the distance, like fleecy clouds banked against the Horizen.[3]

We traveled 20 miles to day. Musketoes and Gnats ad-libitum[.]

---

[1] Perhaps the earliest description of Courthouse Rock is by the Rev. Samuel Parker, who saw it in 1835: "It has, at the distance of the width of the river, all the appearance of an old enormous building, somewhat delapidated; but still you see the standing walls, the roof, the turrets, embrasures, the dome, and almost the very windows . . ." (*Journal of an Exploring Tour beyond the Rocky Mountains*, p. 64).

[2] West of Courthouse Rock stands Chimney Rock, looking very much like an upside down funnel. Alonzo Delano, who saw it in 1849, left the following description: "The rock much resembled the chimney of a glass-house furnace. A large cone-like base, perhaps a hundred and fifty feet in diameter, occupied two thirds of its height, and from thence the chimney ran up, gradually growing smaller to the top. . . . It is a great curiosity" (*Across the Plains and Among the Diggings*, p. 26).

Emigrants were often deceived as to the distance of such objects. Caroline Richardson remarked, for example: "rose early as we contemplated a visit to chimney rock we were however detained and did not go which was quite lucky for us as it took no less than nine miles drive to bring us opposite to it[.]" Later she commented: "it can be seen at a great distance resembling a high factory chimney but as you approach it assumes an apperance [*sic*] of a strong fortification   there are several structures of the same material and of every variety of shapes   it seems as if nature had employed her best architects to lay out and execute the fictious [*sic*] piece of work so strikingly beautiful, and yet so deceiving   it is covered with names and is visited every day by a great many who add to the list" ("Journal and Commonplace Book," p. 52). Howard Stansbury describes it at some length and gives James Bridger's opinion ". . . that it was reduced to its present height by lightning, or some other sudden catastrophe, as he found it broken on his return from one of his trips to St. Louis, though he had passed it uninjured on his way down" (*Expedition to the Valley of the Great Salt Lake*, p. 51). See also Merrill J. Mattes, "Chimney Rock and the Oregon Trail," *Nebraska History*, XXXVI, 1-26.

[3] Caroline Richardson noted that Scotts Bluff "had been in sight nearly two days" (*op. cit.*, p. 53).

**Wednesday JUNE 2nd**   A pleasant day, with a very good road.

Scott's Bluffs this morning looked to be about ten miles up the river from us; We have traveled, say 20 miles and are not yet up to the Bluffs, lacking some miles, I won't say how far, guessing at distance here is the most complete Hornswaggling game that a man ever undertook. The bottom here is much wider than usual, being from three to five miles wide on either side from the river to the Bluffs[.] A light shower of rain fell this afternoon, after which, the wind rose and blew for all that was out — giving us a specimen of a Platte river storm of wind. Now while writing, siting [*sic*] in the wagon the wind rocks me so that I can hardly write legably[.] In the present view, we have two ranges of Bluffs on the north side, the second, being far, far beyond the first range, towering high, with uneaven ragged outlines, looking like a bank of 2 clouds consulting the propriety of raining[.]

**Thursday JUNE 3rd**   Rain during last night and this morning until about 9 O-clock. After the rain seaced we hooked up & drove some 7 miles & nooned on the bank of Coal Creek, during the forenoon's drive we passed Scott's Bluffs, one of the most beautiful sights that I ever saw in the shape of rock & earth, they tower high, with Gigantic Grandure, the dops [*sic*; tops] & sides of some being studed with Cedars looking like an old cultivated Nursery.[4] We traveled this afternoon, say 6 miles making in all 13 miles for the whole day. The bottom to day seemed much wider than at any other point being say from one to 8 or 10 miles wide[.] Buffalo shit very scarce   not enough to cook with   bad times for some thing to eat, — though very good grazing for the stock. I feel some tired of this Platte river, a change in name would be some relief, I hope to find wood tomorrow, and have some bean soupe, good fresh bread, stewed fruit &c[.] This will do — yes, yes;

[4] Traveling on the north side of the river, Wayman's party crossed the site now occupied by the city of Scottsbluff, Nebraska. Southwest across the river is Scotts Bluff National Monument, commemorating the historic associations of this place.

JUNE 1 - JUNE 30, 1852

Lydia Rudd's reaction to seeing the bluffs is typical of that of most emigrants: ". . . they are the most interesting of anything of that [sort] I have seen yet I was delighted with the view from where we have encamped. . . . They extended for miles looking like a city of ruined castles churches towers monuments assuming all shapes and forms . . . towering to a height of two or three hundred feet . . ." (Diary for June 11; no pagination). For the earliest published account of how Scotts Bluff received its name, see Washington Irving, *The Adventures of Captain Bonnville*, pp. 29–30. See also Merrill J. Mattes, *Scotts Bluff National Monument*, and Mattes, "Hiram Scott, Fur Trader," *Nebraska History*, XXVI, 127–62. Platt and Slater, *Travelers' Guide*, devote a half page to describing Scotts Bluff.

**Friday JUNE 4th 52** To day was clear and very warm — Made an early start & drove slowly, say 10 miles & nooned, in sight of Laramie Peak, which is said to be over one hundred miles distant.[5] This Peak, from this point looks like a dark cloud resting against the western Horizon. This sight, is my first view of the Rocky Mountains; Though very small in appearance, it looks Grand — Magnificent — Splendid. We this evening have found wood, and are now making rapid demonstrations towards a good supper, at least, every move looks significant that way. This evening finds us about twenty two miles from our last Camping ground[.] From this point I suppose it to be about twenty miles to Fort Laramie, which place we will reach tomorrow, if no preventing Providence. The Bluffs being near the road to day I visited them & found numerous specimens of various kinds of rock, Among which I found for the first time on this road, large Massive Sand Stone; and a peculiar kind of Grass, which I will recognize, for the want of a more scientific name under the name of Porcupine or Devils grass[.]

---

[5] Wayman's estimate is from Platt and Slater: ". . . a high mountain among the Black Hills, over 100 miles distant. Its height is 6,500 feet above the sea" (p. 8). Laramie Peak, actually 10,272 feet in elevation, is the highest point in the Laramie Mountains. It is about thirty-five miles south of Douglas, Wyoming.

**Saturday JUNE 5th** A cool pleasant morning, journied 11 miles and nooned near the river bank plenty of good wood. No change in the scenery save the Bluffs assume a more Mountainous appearance & Timber more plenty — A drive of 8 miles this afternoon finds [us] encamped on the river bank[6] nearly opposite the celebrated Fort Laramie[.] At a distance the Fort reminds me strongly of little burgs in the States[;] it looks quite cheering to something like civilization in this Wild region of fun and Frollic[.][7]

---

[6] Their camp was presumably on the north side of the North Platte. Fort Laramie is located on the left bank of Laramie Creek near its junction with the North Platte.

[7] The original Fort Laramie was established as a fur trading post in 1834 by William Sublette and Robert Campbell. Later rebuilt by the American Fur Company, the fort was taken over as a military post by the U.S. Government in 1846–47 to protect emigrants. See LeRoy R.

Hafen and Francis M. Young, *Fort Laramie and the Pageant of the West;* Remi Nadeau, *Fort Laramie and the Sioux Indians;* and David L. Hieb, *Fort Laramie National Monument.* Platt and Slater give the distance from Fort Kearney as "over 337 miles" (p. 8).

Many 1852 emigrants described the fort in their diaries, which convey their reactions to this remote outpost of civilization. Silas V. Miller, for example, wrote: ". . . there was a store, a grocery Several dwellings . . . and Soldiers Quarters, which was a long Shed or Stable appearing building, and the Magazine house[.] The Fort is a long, hollow Square about 30 ft high and walls about 20 Inches thick built of sunburnt bricks, three or 4 cannon mounted on the walls, there are Several Small Rooms on the inside of this Square, and a kind of a poarch on the inside . . . 4 or 5 ft of the top so wide that six men can walk in a breast" (Letter to his brother; Salem, Nov. 24, 1852, pp. 8–10.

After traveling up the dreary monotony of the Platte valley, most emigrants, like Wayman, looked forward to their arrival at Fort Laramie. A sense of what they felt is conveyed by G. A. Smith, who wrote in his diary, ". . . who can describe the travlers feelings on arriving at this place inhabited by white people[?] . . . I heard the cow bells ring as I came in sight" (no pagination. Entry for May 13).

**Sunday June 6th**   Last evening we had a specimen of a Platte river hail storm, it was Kept up for two hours; Well it was one of them. This morning was cool and fine, quite a cool breeze all day. We are lying in Camp to day, to rest our animals. This morning I wrote a letter to J. V. Wayman crossed the river and went to the Fort. They have almost every thing for sale that one may want, but at enormous prices.[8]

For instance ten dollars and fifty cents per hundred, for flour, and all else in proportion. It looks quite wholesome to see houses and stables, and respectable looking Gents and Ladies.

From here, we can see an other Mountain range in addition to Laramie peak. The river at this place is quite norrow [sic], not being more than three hundred years wide, but very deep[.]

The Bluffs ahead of us are very high and mountain like, being studed over with Cedar & pine; in the distance they look beautiful and Grand. The grass here is quite short — Plenty of good wood, and old rich muddy filthy Platte water. Here we are, shure, certain.

---

[8] Emigrants could replenish their supplies at the sutler's store, which still stands. Lucy R. Cooke said her husband bought lemon syrup, preserved quinces, chocolate, seidlitz powders, candy sticks, and "other goodies" as well as ink. "He says it's a splendid store . . . and it was crowded with people, and clerks were as busy as at any large city store" (*Crossing the Plains in 1852,* p. 29).

Like Wayman, Thomas Turnbull also thought that prices were high: "At the Fort Hard bread $13 pr C.  Loaf bread worth 10 cts in Chicago 60 cts. here.  Tobaco [sic] 6ˢ per lb. Vinegar $2 pr Gallon   Tea $2 pr lb.   everything very dear" (*Travels from the United States . . . ,* p. 171). Others, like A. M. Crane, thought prices were reasonable. He bought a pair of mocassins from a French Canadian for only $1.00 ("Journal . . . ," p. 29). Mary

S. Bailey bought sugar and raisins for fifty cents a pound, salaratus (*i.e.*, soda) for seventy-five cents, and a "paper of tacks" for eighty cents ("Journal," p. 10).

**Monday JUNE 7th 1852** A cool fresh morning — after traveling some five miles, we left the vally and went into the hills.— Found them high rough & rugged,[9] though most beautiful to view, being clothed in many places with Cedar & pine. Here I found a specimen of pure Native Mica, & clean Mica Slate rock, crystalized Quartz, petrified wood of various shapes, & the red Sand stone in massive quantities. This was a rich treat to me, having been worn out with so much sameness along the Platte[.] at 3 Oclock this evening we found a first rate spring of cold sweet water. Here we rested, filled our vessels, & comenced our Mountain like journey; the evening found us to the river again. Plenty of good dry pine wood and has been for some day[s] now and I trust will still be the case, long as consistant with the nature of things. We have traveled over about twenty two miles of Terrefirma, and that rough as you could wish[.] Grazing tolerably good in places. Quite cool nights these are, cold enough to beare two blankets and a Buffaloe rug.

[9] "It is quite a distance threw [*sic*] those hills," wrote E. B. Mapel; "they are verry Rough & High & not much grass[.] we made generaly a 100 miles a week" ([Account of experiences crossing the plains . . .], p. 5).

**Tuesday JUNE 8th** A cool clear day; fine for traveling. The road to day lay over long sloping hills, with the exception of two steep abrupt places, the road to day was tolerably easy and firm. About 8 Oclock we came to and passed down a long norrow valley between high rocky mountain like hills, presenting a scenery in point of variety and grandure beyond any thing of the kind, that I ever saw heard or read of. Since we left Laramie, the wild sage is quite plenty; in places the surface of the ground is covered for acres[.][10]

To night finds us encamped, without wood or water; being the first time that such an occurance has befallen us, and this was wholly unnecessary; but for our guide,[11] who did not fully understand his business. This afternoon passed some Indian tents, where we saw specimens of Indian men Squaws, Young Squaws and Children,[12] of whom I baught a pair of Moccasins, I put them on immediately, and cut a gash, I did. Traveled in all to day, probably 22 miles. Mc wanted very badly to camp near the Indian tents, for wat reasons, he yet refuses to tell.

[10] Discarded belongings also lay scattered over much of the ground. "It is quite common now," wrote Caroline Richardson on June 16, "to see beds and bedding by the roadside which some have discarded to lighten their loads and some because they had been the couch of sickness and death, in some places the ground is strewed with male and female attire which indicates that the presence of the grim monster has been felt" ("Journal and Commonplace

Book," p. 67). That same day her company passed five new graves and also saw some men digging another one for a young girl.

[11] This is the only indication that the Wayman party employed a guide.

[12] These may possibly have been the same Indians whom Mary S. Bailey described: ". . . it was realy a great curiosity to see so many at home — they are very indolent but healthy look[ing] hardy & [one word illegible] of ordinary fat[i]gue [?] should think theyre was 200 from on old blind woman to a little baby not more than 9 days old all sorts & sizes[.] A trader lives with them, will not let them sell a pony without his consent — one old man has been to Washington they all wore rings on their wrists & on every finger — some of the Children were white enough to belong to any white family —" ("Journal," p. 11).

**Wednesday JUNE 9th 1852** Quite a respectable day this, made a short drive say twelve miles. We drove about 5 miles this fore noon & came to the river where we nooned. A train drove near us while in camp and Kicked up a fight up [sic] among themselves making a regular dog time, indeed such actions belong to brutes, not men. While men act like men, especially when on a trip like this, they always find enough to do, to the entire exclusion of such senseless brutality, alas, but few seem to appreciate this truth[.]

From where we are now encamped, can be seen a range of Mountains[13] extending north from Laramie Peak for more than one hundred miles, looking like a bank of dark blue clouds forming the western horizon. The river here is quite norrow, not being more than two or three hundred yards wide, and skirted with wood enough for our purposes. The road to day has been very good, but few hills & firm. Grazing very good. We had a first rate pot of bean soupe to day, and pies; and from the promtings of my stomach they will be fully appreceated I think[.]

[13] An extension of the Laramie Mountains. Their northernmost extremity is Haystack Range and Deer Creek Range south of Casper, Wyoming.

**Thursday JUNE 10th 1852** Our road this day lay over a tolerably smoothe firm rolling plain, — during the afternoon we assended a very high rocky hill, which in decending was the most abrupt and steep decent that we have yet made. In all to day we have traveled over probably 18 miles, encamping on the bank of the river, in the most beautiful groves of timber that I have seen since we have been journeying westward. Numerous large Cotton Wood trees, of which some are dry supplying us with good fier wood and of which we are making good use ————

This Camp ground has been the site recently of a temporary Indian Vilage of which we have numerous evedinces, in the shape of old Moccasins, poles, forks, and bones. This evening threatens rain, but it seems disposed to pass around us. A party of our train took a hunt to day and was luckey enough to kill two Antelope, which will serve us with fresh meat sufficient at least for the present. I feel a strange inclination to taste some of the *"animule"* myself "I do." Grass here is not very good, which is the only objection that could be urged against this ground ————

**Friday JUNE 11th** A very windy dry day, started at 5 Oclock this morning went on to the bluffs and encauntered [sic] some of the roughest road that we have yet seen, About 9 Oclock neared the river again & nooned in the bottom. This forenoon, while rambling among the Cliffs, I found a beautiful specimen of pure Native Feldspar, among a mass of brown Massive Sand stone, after which, found a quantity of dark brown Soap stone, intersperced with a white metalic looking Mineral, easily broken with a short granular fracture.

17 — miles to day

While resting on the bank of the river, saw a large Buffaloe bull on the opposite shore, say four hundred yards distant, he was a fine specimen of his kind. The road this afternoon was quite sandy in places making it very heavy wheeling: with this exception the road was level and firm. The evening finds us again on the Platte's bank, without any change in the scenery, though some change in my feelings. I begin to feel very anxious to get among the Rocky Mountains, where I expect to find quite an interesting change from anything I have yet seen[.]

**Saturday JUNE 12th** A very windy dry dusty day, though cool and fine in other respects — Most of the road to day was very sandy and consequently tiersom traveling. Notwithstanding we are now in port without the loss of one, and preparing the needful rest. During our peregrinations to day we may have passed over near 18 miles, passing what is called the lower ferry,[14] where the remains of an old bridge is yet to be seen. Here we found some emigrants of whom we baught some salt at the rate of 5 dollars per bushel, and priced their Mercy drops, which was only estimated to be worth 8 dollars per gallon, this a quality [sic] that did not quite suit us, we most respectfully declined buying any. A species of the Cactus for several days past seem to be the principal production of the soil. Wood and Platte water plenty yet[.] Deer and Antelope plenty among the bluffs; and notwithstanding the repeated invitations, they have up to the present time (with one exception) refused to show themselves in Camp, this I think is not treating gentlemen with due respect.

---

[14] The term *lower ferry* is from Platt and Slater (p. 11). If the mileage which they give is accurate, this ferry was several miles south of Douglas, Wyoming. Wayman's party had presumably continued their journey on the north side of the river because none of the place names which Platt and Slater list between Fort Laramie and the lower ferry appears in Wayman's diary.

**Sunday JUNE 13th 1852** This morning we hooked up and drove some three or four miles to a good Camping and grazing place and stoped for the day. We have no preaching, though we have a Minister in our company. If we do not serve our Maker directly with flattering songs of adulation and humble petitions for kind rememberances and favors, we do so quite as acceptably to Him & agreeably to my self, resting ourselves & animals and providing for the further prossec[u]tion of our Journey[.] Fine grazing and good wood in a grove of Cotton wood on the river bank, where we are to day in Camp respectfully assembled, in the faithful discharge of our respective duties, Save Our Minister who has seen fit to make a wash day of this, and still refuses to grant a dispensation to common sinners, that they might step down into [the] pool while the waters are troubled and be clensed on this good Lord's day. To morrow I expe[c]t that we will arrive at the ferry, and pass it. Then we lean for Independence Rock.

**Monday JUNE 14th 1852** Quite a cool day, drove about 18 miles, and camped without wood or water, and very slim grazing[.] We carried water from the river for cooking and drinking purposes. We passed the ferry[15] this after noon about 4 Oclock, and found squads of wagons on both sides of the river, those on the south side, taking their regular turns ferrying across. Saw Fritters the size of your hand selling for a dime apiece, Whiskey selling at 25 cents a drink, two dollars & 25 cents per pint or 8 dollars per gallon[.][16]

We here leave[17] the Platte river for the last time, and have a drive of 26 miles to make before we find water fit to drink for man or beast.[18] We hope to make it tomorrow. The Valley up here is norrowed down to a very small concern in comparison, and the bluffs are quite Mountain like on the south side and studed over with Cedar and pine: While the Mountains[19] in the distance towering high and dark against the Heavens present a Sublime view[.] We are having a cold Mountain air now, and will have. We are approaching very near the old Mountains in person[.]

---

[15] The upper ferry; also known as the Mormon ferry. Writing in her diary on June 18, Lodisa Frizzell noted that there were three boats "well fixed with ropes & pullies" which were operated "by some french, & Indians" (*Across the Plains to California*, p. 26). Ferriage was five dollars per wagon and fifty cents for each animal and human being. At this rate, profits were impressive, for Jared Fox on June 11 counted two hundred teams waiting and approximately four thousand additional animals ("Memorandum," p. 18). When water was low, emigrants could ford the river at two or three places and thus avoid ferriage (Platt and Slater, p. 11). The ferry was located at what is today Casper, Wyoming. Crossing from the south to the north side of the river, emigrants left the North Platte west of there and struck out for the Sweetwater River.

[16] Frizzell says that " a frenchman . . . kept a few articles to sell, the principle article was whiskey, which he sold at 12 dollars per gallon, or 25 cts a drink" (*op. cit.*, p. 25).

[17] The use of *leave* instead of *cross* reinforces the idea that Wayman's party had come up the north side of the river.

[18] Platt and Slater warned: "You will find no good water . . . for 22 miles. . . . You will find some which is very poisonous, on account of the immense amount of alkali in this region. Thousands of cattle and horses have died here from drinking the water. Keep your stock from this water or you will lose your teams" (p. 11). Similar warnings appear in other guide books.

[19] Rattle Snake Range

**Tuesday JUNE 15th**  Our road to day lay over long sloping hills, and very hard and firm.[20] Wood very scarce indeed none at all[.] we have now to resort to sage bushes for fier, which answers a tolerably good purpose, quite good as Buffaloe shit. The country presents quite a barren appearance, being no timber in sight to day, and a boundless view with the Mountains in the far distance. I expect that we will find the sweet water river tomorrow, where I hope to fare better. The water for fifty miles back has been strongly Alkaline[.]
  26 miles to day traveled

[20] On June 11, Jared Fox wrote in his diary that the road was mostly uphill but in good condition. Some miles beyond the upper ferry, he found many abandoned possessions: ". . . wagon irons, stoves, and furniture, overcoats, bed clothes, 1 bed of feathers, hats, coats, boots, and all sorts. Bones and graves" ("Memorandum," p. 18).

**Wednesday JUNE 16th**  A fine white Frost this morning, quite cold night.[21] Hooked up early this morning and commenced our perigrenations for the day, passing over a tolerably level road, though very sandy one half of the time. Saw a herd of Buffaloe this fore noon, feeding leisurely along the foot of the Bluffs: did not disturb them, I judge it to be an unproffitable occupation at least for me to follow[.] About ½ past two Oclock we came to the Sweet Water River, and watered our stock.[22] The independence Rock being near the road side, I left the teams and assended the rock, which is composed of Mica Felspar and Quartz, being genuine Granite. This rock is said to be 140 rods long and 120 feet high, it is a splendid site to visit.[23] After leaving the rock we came to the river again & crossed it on a log ferry boat[24] and are now encamped on the south side. The Mountain like peaks surrounding here look in the distance like Pure Granite[.] The water in the Sweet Water is cool and good coming directly from the Mountains [.] Traveled to day about 20 miles all told.

[21] There was a frost on the night of June 15/16. Jared Fox found ice in his dishes.

[22] They reached the Sweetwater approximately twenty miles west of Alcova, Wyoming. The Sweetwater, a stream of clear water having its source in the southern watershed of the Wind River Mountains, flows in an easterly direction until it joins the North Platte at Pathfinder Reservoir. Following it, emigrants headed directly toward South Pass at the Continental Divide.

[23] Independence Rock lies adjacent to Wyoming State Highway 220 about twenty miles east of its junction with U.S. 287. One can easily climb it from the east side. Wayman's figures as to its size, which he copied from Platt and Slater (p. 12), are greatly exaggerated. Frémont measured it in 1842 and gave its length as 650 yards and its height as forty feet (J. C. Fré-

mont, *Report of the Exploring Expedition to the Rocky Mountains in the Year 1842 . . . ,* p. 56). See Robert Spurrier Ellison, *Independence Rock, the Great Record of the Desert.*

The first white men known positively to have seen this famous landmark were a small group of fur traders led by Robert Stuart in the employ of John Jacob Astor. They passed it on October 29, 1812. See Washington Irving, *Astoria,* p. 490n. Trappers and emigrants later recognized it as an ideal camp site, and many who stopped inscribed or painted their names on the rock. Father De Smet, who visited it in 1840, called it "the great registry of the desert" (*Letters and Sketches,* reprinted in *Early Western Travels,* XXVII, 162).

Lodisa Frizzell, five days after Wayman's visit, wrote: "There are thousands of names of persons upon this rock, which have been placed there from year to year, by those who think, 'there is something in a name . . .'" (*op. cit.,* 27). Thomas Turnbull also stated that "Almost this entire stone is covered with dates & the names of visitors painted thereon with red, white black etc." (*Travels from the United States . . . ,* p. 176). Enoch Conyers wrote that ". . . names were written with white or red chalk; some were cut in the rock with a cold chisel, whilst others were written with tar — and, in fact, were written in every conceivable manner" ("Diary," p. 454). Some emigrants, he reported, even searched the rock for names of friends or relatives who had already traveled here in previous years. Today most of these names have been obliterated by time and the elements, but some are still visible on the north and south ends. Emigrants who camped at Independence Rock, one of them reported, ". . . Build Shades and Roast Buffalow & antelope & have a Jolley Good time of it" (E. B. Mapel, [Account of experiences crossing the plains], p. 5). See also Algeline Ashley, "Diary," p. 4; Jared Fox, *op. cit.,* p. 18, who recorded a wedding here on June 12; Alpheus Graham, "Journal," p. 11; Hosea B. Horn, *Horn's Overland Guide,* p. 23; Platt and Slater, p. 12; and Mrs. Francis Sawyer, *Overland to California,* p. 8.

24 The width and depth of the Sweetwater varied with the year and the season. In July, 1849, James F. Wilkins reported it to be only one and one-half feet deep and twenty feet wide (*An Artist on the Overland Trail,* p. 53), but in June of that same year James Pritchard said that the channel was sixty to eighty feet wide and also deep (*Overland Diary,* p. 91). A ferry, consequently, might well have been needed when Wayman reached the Sweetwater.

**Thursday JUNE 17th** Drove about five miles to day, and put up to recruit our stock finding good grass and water[.] We are encamped near the Devil's Gate one of the greatest natural curiosities that I ever saw, or expect ever to see. It is some 50 rods in length and say 300 feet on either side perpendicular in hight, and probably not more than 100 feet wide, these natural battlements are of genuine Granite, presenting the most gigantic, grand and awfully sublime appearance that I ever beheld —[25] Indeed all the mountains that we have seen since we arrived at the Independence rock are principally formed of Granite. The five miles that we traveled over to day lay between two ranges of Granite cliffs or Mountains. The road was the finest that I ever saw any where being a genuine Pike formed from disintegrated granite rock, this was rather extravigant I will admit, but I felt equal to the task. The morning being fine and balmy and traveling along a splendid granite pike road[.]

I felt splendid, I enjoyed my self fully, yes I felt Heavenly. I *do* think that after looking over all my past life, I could call to mind no period in life in which

## JUNE 1 - JUNE 30, 1852

I ever enjoyed myself quite as fully as I did on this said morning, indeed I kept it up during the whole day, and am not quite over the spell this evening while writing. I assended the mountains to day in search of specimens such as might happen in my way, and was richly rewarded for my trouble — I found one mountain spurr formed of Granite and Gniess rocks in partnership, this new to me and very grand and interesting. during my peregnnations [*sic*] to day I found some beautiful specimens of Mica Schist, crystalized Quartz, pure gniess, and all colors and varieties of Granite some tinged with Actinolite most beautifully[.] Take it all around the room[,] I have spent this good day very very pleasantly, I think that I could spend ten days here proffitably. I am shure they would be spent agreeably to me. The mountains in the distance ahead look s[t]ill more gigantic and ruged, fine, double fine.

[25] Devil's Gate, about five or six miles farther west, is visible from Independence Rock. Wayman's figures are from Platt and Slater (p. 12), except that he changed *four hundred* to *three hundred*. This gap, through which the Sweetwater flows, is a short distance north of Highway 220, which at this location lies on the actual route of the old trail.

**Friday JUNE 18th** A dry fine day, our road lay up the Sweet Water valley, level but very heavy and sandy. The Mountains on the north side of the river, are entirely bare nothing to be seen, but occasionally a feiw Cedar or pine bushes, they look grey, uneaven and rugged[.] While they are all covered on the south side with soil and vegetation in the shape of grass Pine and Cedar bushes. The bottom is so far sandy, very deep the worst that we have yet seen and literally covered with Sage bushes. This evening M Shearer killed an Antelope. Good, Good. Tr. 21 miles.

**Saturday JUNE 19th** Same kind of weather to day being dry, sandy very sandy, dusty warm and windy. This is hard on the eyes, yes Develish disagreeable but have to stand it, all right. No wood, but sage bushes and Buffaloe shit[.] This Sweet Water river aught to have been called Crooked river[.] it is the most winding[,] crooked, and twisting little streams [*sic*] that I ever saw[.] It is not more than fifty feet wide, and fordable for a horse in most places,[26] but generally too deep for a wagon[.] We traveled 18 miles to day, and are now in Camp[.]

[26] Horn's *Overland Guide* mentions five fords east of Ice Slough and four others west of there.

**The Lord's Day JUNE 20th** Well, we traveled to day if it was Sunday, about 21 miles over a very sandy road. Yet very dry and dusty. Very disagreeable indeed[.] We left the bottom this morning and assended and desended hill after hill until near night, and arrived at the river again, all being very tired. Nothing unusual occured to day save the Snow Caped Mountains in the (not far) distance[.] I think that we will be among them next day after tomorrow[.] Here we forded the river, & found it quite easy, much more so than was expected. The Bluffs here on both side are comparatively low and wave like; — This scenery reminds me of the old Platte again. Well we are creeping along slowly, and will soon have passed the Rocky Mountains, at least the long remembered South-Pass. The nights here are very cold requiring some care to keep warm — Though the days are very warm, from 10 A.M. until 3 in the afternoon. The mornings and evenings are quite fine and pleasant. The boys Killed another Antelope last evening[.] Fresh meat is the order of the day[.]

**Monday JUNE 21st**   Started at 5 Oclock this morning and found the road stretching over the Bluffs, which were very steep and long — came to the river and nooned. Took up our line of march again and passed over over [sic] a beautiful region of the country, with the exception of a fiew rocky hills just as bad as they well could be, however the balance of the way was comparatively very good, During the after noon we were attracted some distance from the road, by a bank of snow packed away very carefully, in a little hallow (I suppose expressly for somer use) which contrasted finely with the warm day and aired appearance of all else.[27] The snow Caped mountains[28] are and have been for two or three days past in full view. We are quite near them now, — they look splendid. From here it is[29] about 17 miles to the summit of the Pass. All the hills that we have [crossed] this afternoon seem to be composed entirely of Gneiss rock sticking their black heads and edges just above the surface of the ground, giving the hills in places quite a black appearance in the distance. We traveled say 24 miles to day, and are encamped on a tributary of the Sweet Water[.]

---

[27] Wayman undoubtedly refers to what emigrants called Ice Slough, a swamp-like area below the surface of which they could dig for ice. Esther Hanna wrote of it: "Came near a large snowbank. I went to it and found it about 3 feet deep, solid snow mixed with ice" (*Canvas Caravans,* p. 57). Lodisa Frizzell on June 25, five days after Wayman was here, also noted in her journal: "We passed a bank of snow, and an ice spring, so called, from its water being as cold as ice could make it. It was excellent water but the weather was rather to[o] cold to have made much of a relish of it" (*op. cit.,* p. 29). Many diarists comment on this phenomenon, which provided them with ice in mid-summer.

By this time, however, cattle were beginning to give out. One day before reaching Ice Slough, Caroline Richardson noted twelve dead oxen and eighteen more the day following (*op. cit.,* p. 80).

[28] The southern extremity of the Wind River Mountains.

[29] The words *we are* are crossed off and replaced by *it is*.

**Tuesday JUNE 22nd**   Found a very good road to day, and a fine day to travel[.] We arrived at Sweet Water about 10 Oclock and nooned. Near 12 Ooclock [sic] we hooked up and commenced our jaunt through the Pass,[30] passing the Summit about 4 Oclock, and encamped near a Spring branch[31] having traveled 21 miles[.] The mountains on both sides towering high, — those to the north[32] being Caped with snow and the intervening valley & surrounding mounds and peaks is most enlivening & heartsom. This suits me, I feel very well[.]

---

[30] South Pass. Although the elevation is 7,550 feet, the ascent is so moderate that travelers were sometimes uncertain as to when they reached the top. Silas V. Miller, for example, remarked: "5th of July we Started on, right up Sweet Water. Still rising till we come to the Summit, the rise to the Summit was so gradual that we could not tell from appearances when were were on the deviding [sic] ridge, though in a mile or 2 we came to what is called the Pacific Springs . . ." (Letter to his brother, Nov. 24, 1852, p. 11). The area is a wide, open plain covered only with sage brush.

[31] Pacific Springs, a marshy area with clear pools of water that form the source of Pacific Creek, a tributary of the Little Sandy. Although great numbers of emigrants camped at Pacific Springs, some found it quite unsuitable for this purpose. Lodisa Frizzell remarked that it was ". . . a poor place to camp, for where there is any grass, it is so miry that it is dangerous for stalk [i.e., stock] to go, 2 or 3 of ours got in the mire & a good many others, they were got out, but with much difficulty" (op. cit., p. 30). John Lewis noted that there were about one hundred wagons near Pacific Springs when he arrived, and because of this his party drove their stock four miles north for better forage ("Diary," pp. 82–83). When A. M. Crane reached the springs on June 27, four days after Wayman, he said that "An endless number have pitched their tents about us" ("Journal," p. 44a).

[32] The Wind River Range. Pacific Butte, which lies in an eastwest direction close to and south of Pacific Springs, obstructs a view of the Uinta Mountains far to the south in Utah. Wayman in saying "the mountains on both sides" probably refers to the Wind River Mountains and to the Salt Range, which lies along the western boundary of Wyoming.

---

**Wednesday JUNE 23rd** This day we remained in camp near Pacific creek[,] which is the first water that emties [sic] into the Pacific Ocean[.] a range of snow caped mountains north west of us, & in the South East a very pretty range of smoothe even Mountains[33] and the intervening valley said to be 30 miles in width, taken all around the room this view is gotten up on a larger and more gigantic scale than any thing that I have yet seen. You can here see at one sight more m[a]gnificence and imposing grandure than common sinners ever dreamed of[.]

I visited the Bluffs to day to see what I could see. Nothing new save an unusaul amount of Mica, entering into the composition of the rocks. The rocks that I examined were A vari[e]ty of Granite and Quartz[,] Red and Green sand stone and some schistose rock[.] A large family of Indians are encamped within 3 hundred yards of us, they are very filthy and hard looking, though peaceable and harmless[.] I have a fine specimen of Mica Hornblend & Quartz in combination to remember the old South Pass[.] This is me I think but am not certain[.]

---

[33] Pacific Butte, which is not really a mountain but a range of hills.

**Thursday JUNE 24th** A cold cloudy day, rained some in the afternoon[.] road fine laying along a smoothe & nearly level plain with mountains on both sides. The wind river Mountains being in the North West,[34] partly covered with snow[.] This is quite an extensive range stretching in a north western direction. This evening finds us encamped on Little Sandy,[35] after traveling near 24 miles[.] Mc & Loring are awful dusty [lusty?] for an Indian frigg[.][36] I pitty them[.] O God I am [one word illegible]

---

[34] Wayman's error for north and northeast.

[35] The Little Sandy and Pacific Creek join three miles east of Farson, Wyoming. Horn's *Overland Guide* describes the Little Sandy as being ". . . 25 feet wide; 2 feet deep. Some timber and grass, and a pretty good place to camp . . ." (p. 29).

[36] Coitus

**Friday, JUNE 25th** To day the road was more uneaven, yet passably good and firm. Grass very scarce & has been for some days past, indeed Wild Barley is our only refuge here at this time, it is excellent good feed, but it so thinly inhabits the earth that we give the *"Animules"* a longer time to finish their repast. Not one stick of timber of any kind in sight, though we get along with Sage bushes. A shower of rain this evening again. I am ready to believe that it rains among the Mountains here every day[.] Traveled to day 20 miles, crossed Big Sandy[37] at 10 Oclock & are encamped in sight of it on the Bluffs[.]

---

[37] The Big Sandy flows southwest into the Green River. Horn's *Overland Guide* describes it as being "8 rods wide; 2 feet deep. Clear, swift current; good crossing, and a good place to camp; you will find no more water for 49 miles" (p. 30).

**Saturday JUNE 26th** A very beautiful blamy [*sic*] morning, hooked up and started at five Oclock, found the road firm and good, though some[38] rolling. We nooned in sight of Big Sandy and within 5 miles of Green river.[39] A range of mountains[40] presented themselves in the South East to day of the most beautiful character — As usual it rained a very little this evening, the heavy part of the rain seemes to be (as it has been for 10 or 15 days back) in the north West. Very cool nights and when clear very warm and oppr[e]ssive during the day from 10 until 2 Oclock[.] Since we left the summit in the South Pass, our road has been along a level plane, between two ranges of Mountains. Crossing during this time we crossed the little and Big Sandy, and[41] Green river. We arrived at and crossed Green river about 3 Oclock, crossing at the Mormon Ferry,[42] this is a little out of the way, but we could not cross at the upper ferry on account of the numbers of wagons waiting. We traveled about 17 miles to day, and are now encamped on the west side of Green River good grass

---

[38] *To* is crossed out after *some*.

[39] Presumably Wayman's party had traveled down the east bank of the Big Sandy, cross

to the west bank after a day's travel of twenty miles from the Little Sandy, and then either followed the river farther or struck out west toward the Green River. Although their exact route is difficult to determine with certainty, it appears that they used what was known as Kinney cutoff, which had the advantage of avoiding the barren, waterless desert traversed farther north by the Sublette cutoff. Wayman's statement that within five miles of the Green they were still in sight of the Big Sandy makes this inference almost inevitable. The most explicit description of the Kinney road is in George R. Stewart's *The California Trail*, p. 304; he says that on this route emigrants followed the Big Sandy but that before it joined the Green, they left it and struck out about ten miles across the angle between them (cf. Enoch Conyers: "Came ten miles to Green River . . ." ["Diary," p. 464]). Crossing the Green on a ferry, or fording it when water was low, they then traveled west, following Slate Creek (cf. Conyers, p. 465) until they reached the main cutoff. Stewart's maps used in preparation for *The California Trail* are deposited in the Bancroft Library at the University of California at Berkeley and have been valuable to me in trying to work out Wayman's route.

Conyers pointed out the advantages of the Kinney cutoff by saying that it was "thirty-three miles nearer than Subletts cut-off and a much better road" (p. 465). For another description of this cutoff by an emigrant, see John McAllister, "Diary," pp. 488–89.

[40] The Uinta Mountains in northeast Utah.

[41] *The* is crossed out after *and*.

[42] Because there was more than one Mormon Ferry, it is not possible to identify the one that Wayman refers to; however, evidence seems to indicate that Wayman's party crossed the Green about ten miles below Fontenelle Dam. This location also corresponds to their probable use of the Kinney cutoff. On July 14, 1852, Enoch Conyers reported two ferries at this crossing of the Green River. Ferriage was three dollars per wagon. The river, he said, was "about seventy-five yards wide" (p. 464).

**Sunday JUNE 27th** The road to day was frequently interupted with short deep gutters making it very disagreeable and tiersom with this exception the road was firm and good[.] From the Mormon ferry where we crossed the river the road lay up the Valley some 10 miles[43] then leaving Green river we assended the Bluffs and traveled say six miles and came to a norrow deep muddy and turbid stream, from which we obtained water for our selves and stock. Again took to the hills and traveled say 4 miles making in all for this good Sunday about 20 miles. Grass quite scarce[.] Once more a little shower of rain, a little Thunder, A little Grass, A little Wood in the shape of Sage[,] A little Water and not very good at that, and Musketoes in any quantity of all sizes ages from the size of a Gnat up to a Humingbird, with their bills all freshly sharpened, and ravinous appitites[.]

[43] Presumably to Slate Creek. Richard O. Hickman (*An Overland Journey to California*, p. 13) and Thomas Turnbull (*Travels from the United States*, p. 181) also mention traveling ten miles up the Green to Slate Creek. Alpheus Richardson crossed the Green on a ferry. "Here we left the Mormon Road and took Kenny [*sic*] new cut off. Followed up the river 10 miles and camped on it. Good roads, grass and wood" ("Diary," p. 12).

**Monday JUNE 28th** A very fine pleasant morning started tolerably early & made a drive of some 10 miles or more over a good easy road, though very dusty and nooned, no grass, did not unhook the stock; fed our own faces a bite and drove on and early in the afternoon commenced assending a long high Mountain,[44] the assent was gradual & easy for a mountain road though some of the desents were very steep and difficult. The worst road this evening that I have yet seen[.] During the after noon we found some Indians, of whom, bought a pair of Moccasins, near some Mountain Springs.[45] We found our way down the west side of the mountain among some springs and good grass, after traveling in all to day 21 miles. The mountain[46] just ahead of us in the West has patches of snow dotted all over the east side, it looks delicious. It did not rain to day, being the first omission of the kind since we arrived in this Mountain country. The Cactus are now in bloom all shades of yellow & red. Loring & Mc were after Indian squaws to day again.

---

[44] Possibly Slate Creek Ridge.

[45] This is probably what Richard O. Hickman refers to as Indian Springs, ". . . a most beautiful spring of pure water flowing from the foot of the mountain" (*op. cit.*, p. 13). This spring lies west of U.S. 189 between Kemmerer and La Barge, Wyoming. On the official Wyoming State Highway Map, where it is labeled Emigrant Springs, it is incorrectly located east of the highway.

[46] Commissary Ridge ?

---

**Tuesday JUNE 29th** Well we had a regular mountain road all day to day — This morning, true[,] the road lay in a narrow valley between two mountain ranges, called the Green River M.s.[47] but I call them and more appropriately too the Sand stone Mns. they being composed allmost entirely of Sand stone so far as I examined. They are generally where we crossed them from 4 to 6 miles over. We have crossed two to day in traveling say 20 miles & it seemed to me as though we were going up or down a mountain all day[.] After traveling some 10 miles this fore noon we came to crossed and nooned at Hams Fork — a branch or Fork of Green River.[48] Hooked up and traveled say 1½ miles and commenced assending a high sloping mountain, over two miles to the summit after which the road was quite good to Aspen grove where we are encamped for the night, having passed over near 20 miles in all to day.[49] Wood & water good, but grass slim. A shower of rain this evening again[.] this is quite a common compliment paid us here in this region[.]

At the south extremity of the grove commences a very deep long valley runing in a south East direction for some miles. it is prehaps [*sic*] a half mile in width at the bottom with steep abrupt walls scarcely accessable at the easyest place for a man.[50] From an eminence on the Battlement any where you can mark the meandering course of the different spring branches[51] that find their way from the banks of the west end of this Grand prospect[.] The southern band is beauti-

JUNE 1 - JUNE 30, 1852

fully studed with young pines[52] of all sizes and shapes arranged in the most splendid order of natural elegance & profusion, while the north side and intervening bottom, are beautifully bedecked with Aspen and Pine bushes, mingled in strange and magnificent elegance, while 5[53] Aged Pines stand up on the northern battlement like so many faithful sentinels watching their most treasured care. Such a scene I never saw before nor need see again to brighten my remembrance of so much Beauty and magnificent Grandure combined. While I think of it and they are yet in sight, I will speak of a Southern range of mountains of the most Splendid character, now while the golden-tinged clouds are hovering in the distance, I can hardly distinguish one from the other. We are here surrounded with almost an unbroken chain of Gigantic M.s. Here I found the most bea[u]tiful flower that I ever saw in my life[.] I mention it to forever Know where I saw so fine a specimen[.] Badgers plenty here, and Mountain squirrels. they live in the ground[.]

[47] The name is now obsolete. The valley lies between Oyster Ridge on the east and Commissary Ridge on the west.

[48] Where Wayman's party crossed Hams Fork, the river flows south-southeast. Many emigrants were impressed by the stream. Esther Hanna, for example, wrote: "Encamped at noon on its banks. It is one of the most enchanting spots I have seen! This is a lovely stream, with gravel bed, beautiful trees, flowers. Here we found our first strawberries. There is an Indian camp here, about 30 wigwams and trading post . . ." (*op. cit.*, p. 62). The Indians were probably Snakes, who wanted to trade fish for bread and fish hooks (Richard O. Hickman, *op. cit.*, p. 13). When Alpheus Richardson was at Hams Fork, he watched ". . . a squaw picking lice off from her papoose's head and eating them as if they were strawberries" ("Diary," p. 13). The bottom land provided lush grass for animals — "the handsomest and longest grass I have seen on the road," wrote Thomas Turnbull; "enough to feed 1000s of Cattle and Horses, this is the place to feed up your teams for 1 week" ("Diary," p. 182). There was also a grave, Jared Fox noted, ". . . marked Leon Balsley, shot June 14th, 1852, for the murder of Matthias Beal, June 12, 1852, both of Boone Co., Kentucky. So justice overtook him soon" ("Memorandum," p. 22). For an account of Beal's murder and Balsley's execution, see Stewart, *The California Trail*, pp. 308–309. A briefer account appears in my introduction; see p. 13.

[49] It appears from what Wayman says here and below that his party had been ascending Hams Fork Plateau leading into the Tump Range, which forms the western watershed of Hams Fork and the divide between it and Bear River. Thomas Turnbull, apparently traveling the same route, wrote: ". . . two roads within a few Rod[s] of each other one going over the mountain Peak & the other round below another hill this misses a good many hills in one ½ Days travel. . . . for all our road struck the Mountain Peak, about the Centre, it is a terrible hill after that we had a road on the top of the Mountains for a long time equal to a turnpike" (*op. cit.*, pp. 182–83).

[50] The phrase *500 feet high* is inserted between lines.

[51] This reference to "different spring branches" can only mean the small creeks feeding into Hams Fork which Wayman, from his "eminence," could see below him as a "Grand Prospect."

[52] *Pines* is followed by an illegible interlinear insertion probably intended to be *& Furr* [fir].

[53] The numeral 5 replaces an illegible word which Wayman crossed out.

**Wednesday JUNE 30th and last.** This was quite a cool fresh morning, everything looked lively and cheerful. I rode back 2 miles to see a sick man and took a last view of my fancied Paradise. I only left this scenery to see orthers [sic] quite as splendid of their Kind. Three miles from our last encampment we came to & passed Fir Grove,[54] of the kind, this is [one of] the most magnificent and romantic spots in the World, from the summit of the mountain west of this Grove, can be seen in all directions gigantic Mountain ranges capped with Eternal snow. The water here is ice cold, & fine[.] From this eminence I can see in various directions everlasting snow hundreds of feet b[e]low me. Of the Kind this cant be beat the World over. The road to day was of the worst possible quality being for miles of rugged assent, and steep long winding and precipitous desents, and all the dust that a strong wind can hold, meeting you in the eyes nose ears mouth and face[.][55] We traveled to day some 15 miles all told[.]

The last mountain that we passed over before reaching Bear river Valley, was composed principally of Pudding stone, Line [sic] stone, Argillaceous and other Kinds of Slate. From this range I obtained a Specimen of what I suppose to be Chrystalized [one word illegible] Lime[.] In this Bear river Valley We find good Wood, Water and grass. We are incamped Very near some very high steep and ruggid mountains[56] which I think of assending to morrow if we lie up here as I think we will[.] Indians plenty here, some fine looking fellows, though generally dirty Snakes[.]

From the commencement of our journey, the diseasess were Diarrhea in two forms, the pale free watery discharges and the Bilious[.] This will be sufficient as a discription, until we left Fort Laramie after which Dyesentery [sic] seemed to take the place of Diarrhea — After reaching the South Pass, we encountered some fever of a Bilious Remittent character, not malignant, being easily controled, when not associated with disease of the Bowels. I have heard of some deaths occuring from this mountain fever,[57] in such cases I think from what I have seen, that it is the result of bad management, and when death does occur,[58] the immediate cause is Peritoneal inflamation. I have visited some cases & indeed the only serious ones were of this character, This induces me to think that all fatal cases terminate in this way. Peritoneal inflamation seems to be a natural concomitant of this Mountain fever. I have seen a number of cases and all seem to weare [sic] this tendency. Though if properly managed there is no danger.

---

[54] Probably the balsam fir grove mentioned in Platt and Slater, p. 16. Turnbull also refers to it: "Balsam fir Grove 3 miles a Tremendous high mountains [sic] the names of 1000s marked on the fir trees here trees 10 to 100 [feet] high . . ." (*op. cit.*, p. 183). John Lewis said that it ". . . is the prittest grove that ever I seen . . ." ("Diary," p. 90), and Jared Fox remarked: ". . . in this grove there is I suppose 5 to 10 thousand . . . names cut in the trees. Some printed with Chalk or waggon grease, red paint and anything and everything. Dates from 1845 to the present, but most in 1850 and many of them are 10 to 15 feet from the ground" ("Memorandum," pp. 22–23).

## JUNE 1 - JUNE 30, 1852

55 Turnbull made the same observation: ". . . then went down some frightful mountains from 1 to 11½ [*sic*] m. pretty near straight about knee deep of fine dust worked so by dregging [*i.e.*, dragging locked wheels] . . ." (*op. cit.*, p. 183). John Lewis ". . . went down about 1½ m. with two wheeles locked. . . . These mountains from Green R. to Bare R. is the worst we have had but here we are in a beautiful valey [Smiths Fork] whare thare is grass anough to feed the world . . ." ("Diary," pp. 90–91). According to Jared Fox, ". . . people tumbled down the hills neck and heels with all the wheels chained mile after mile and then up and down again" ("Memorandum," p. 23).

56 Cokeville Butte and Station Butte adjacent to U.S. 30N twenty miles north of Sage, Wyoming. Through the narrow gap between them runs Smiths Fork, a tributary of Bear River. Hickman also mentions passing through here: ". . . passed through what is termed the Narrows, which are two large Bluffs, one on either side of the road . . ." (*An Overland Journey to California,* pp. 13-14). This point marked the western terminus of the Sublette cutoff, which now met the trail coming up from Fort Bridger.

57 Probably Rocky Mountain spotted fever, caused by the bite of infected ticks, which are prevalent in the mountains during the spring and early summer months. Until recent years, spotted fever was usually fatal. Tick fever, in contrast, is not fatal but causes debilitating symptoms and fever in the victim. See George W. Groh, *Gold Fever,* p. 115.

58 Following *occur,* the words *it is brought about* are crossed out.

# July 1 – July 31, 1852

**Thursday July 1st, 1852** This good July day we are yet in camp[;] the morning[1] passed away while we were suning our goods and chattles. We are situated on the bank of Smith's fork of Bear river in the Bear river Valley about one mile from the river.[2] The valley here is about three miles wide. The mountains in our immediate vicinity are very steep rugged and high; almost entirely composed of Trap rock[.] This is again somthing new to me. A little Cotton Wood, Willow & Haw just where we are along the river[.]

This afternoon I visited an Indian village and baught a good pair of Moccasins. They had 7 skin tents and as many famalies, in the whole, presenting all specimens from the most dirty ragged and filthy creatures up to some very fine looking men and squaws. These are the most noble looking Indians that I have yet seen[.] They are sharp traders. Indians and Musketoes[3] are very plenty[.] Loring & Mc have been missing in the direction of the Indian tents, for what purpose I am unable to say and they refuse to tell, it look[s] quite suspicious[.] [One statement blurred and illegible.]

---

[1] *Has* is crossed out following *morning*.

[2] Their camp was a mile north of Cokeville, Wyoming, on a site midway between where the Union Pacific Railroad and U.S. 30N are now located. Smiths Fork flows from the east into Bear River, which here flows north.

[3] Mrs. Francis Sawyer wrote that at Smiths Fork ". . . the mosquitoes were so thick, so brave and resolute, that all our time was occupied in fighting them off. I never saw the like before . . ." ("Overland to California," p. 10).

**Friday JULY 2nd** A very cold Bear river morning. Crossed Smith Fork of Bear river, at three different branches or prongs within 5 hundred yards travel. just opposite a very high ruggid mountain,[4] stony yes very stony, in the distance this mountain look[s] like a mammoth Edifice Studed over with turrets[.] Thise [*sic*] rock are of the Trap family, or more properly Basalt rock. We traveled down[5] Bear river valley about 8 miles and came to a bridge over Toms Fork[6]

62

of Bear river near 4 miles below the old ford or crossing.[7] Leaving this Toms Fork some three miles; came to a small branch[8] in a norrow Valley between two mountains about 5 Oclock in the evening and encamped for the night. Grass and water very good, but no wood scarcely at all. The Bear river valley is the richest soil that I have seen since I left the states. The mountains are Gigantic & Grand[.] The first Mountain west of the B Valley is principally made of Argillac[e]ous Slate. the decomposed particles make the road here a perfect Slate pike[.] Indeed it is not a very uncommon thing to find short pieces of natural Pike road. I have seen some much superior to any that I ever saw any where else[.] On this rout I have seen Granite Pike of the first water Gneiss pike, Trap pike Basalt Pike and Slate Pike. This is the easiest country to make good pike roads in, that the world can produce. We have traveled in all to day about 12 miles all told[.]

---

[4] Cokeville Butte, extending north of Smiths Fork and east of Bear River.

[5] That is, north.

[6] Thomas Fork flows south through several branches into Bear River near the Wyoming-Idaho north-south boundary. Other diarists also mention the bridge, which Mrs. Francis Sawyer said was a toll bridge. Cost per wagon was one dollar. According to her diary, there was also a ford eight miles from the bridge (*ibid.*, p. 11).

[7] *One* is crossed out following *crossing*.

[8] Sheep Creek, an intermittent stream flowing south into Bear River in Idaho.

**Saturday JULY 3rd** Ice and frost this morning, though quite pleasant in other respects. We drove over a very long high winding mountain and a tortuous road[9] corresponding with said Mountain. This mountain was composed of a kind of Basa[l]tic rock and Slate, after traveling say 8 miles we came to Bear River Valley again traveling up this valley some 6 or 7 miles nooned upon the bank of a small stream[10] running into Bear River, hooked up near 2 Oclock, and made our way up or rather down the valley for 10 miles and camped on a small Spring branch coming directly from the mountains. No Wood nearer than the foot of the mountain. It look[ed] to be near a half mile, and we concluded to walk to the mountain and git a turn of wood apiece, & we found it to be only 2½ miles out, making 5 miles travel for an arm full of wood, after traveling some 25 miles before camping, gras[s] not very good, water fine, that will do[.]

---

[9] *To* is crossed out after *road*.

[10] An unnamed intermittent creek, as is the stream mentioned later in this sentence.

**Forth of JULY 1852** This was a very fine pleasant morning[.] After leaving Ashlie Creek[11] some three miles we passed over a long hill,[12] though not very bad and came to Bear River valley again and kept down this valley in sight of the river until we arrived at the Mineral Springs,[13] where we found a trading shanty[14] kept by some Americans, and numerous Indian Wigwams scattered in all directions.[15] Thes[e] Springs are the greatest Natural curiosities that I ever saw. We encamped here for the night. The first Springs we came to were on an elevated table of White lime like schist rock elevated say 15 or 20 feet above the surrounding plain, upon the summit of which was a small Crater 6 feet in diameter and say five feet deep. Just a feiw feet from this was a spring of water boiling from a small mound the size of a Hamper basket strongly impregnated with Oxide of Iron lime and carbonic acid gass if any thing else I am unable to detect it, this one as well as three other small ones on this eminence were about 98° in temperature.

Just above the last named Mound and to the right about 300 yards is the Kettle Spring, the top of which is three feet from the level and near 4 feet in diameter at the mouth widening out to some 6 feet feet [sic] or more, from the top or brim it is 18 inches to the water which is constantly in agitation from the escape of Carbonic Acid gass. The water looks as though it were boiling. this water is cold and of a strong metalic pungent taste, resembling Still beer more than any thing else, & just to the right of this a fiew paces is another small one boiling up mixed with a fine red earth, looking like red paint. the agitation of the water keeps it well mixed. About 1 mile below may be found several Springs of the same character. ½ mile lower down, is What is known by the name of Steamboat Spring. You can see the water boiling up at a considerable distance, out of the solid rock, the water of this spring is 100° and of the same character as the others, indeed all of these Springs are alike in character, differing only in Strength[.][16]

The Mountains around are very high and rugged being Capped with snow and thier sides decked with Cedar & pine. The rocks forming these Ms. are Trap & Basalt. You can find scattered all around this region an abundance of Scoria & Valcanic rocks[.] The Valley just here between the Mountain & river is intersperced with numerous Cedar groves of the most beautiful kind[.] near the Steamboat Spring are banks of fine Yellow Ocher Natural [material?]. About 3 Oclock in the evening the wind blew a hurricane & about 5 it rained quite hard, and very cold[.] Within in [sic] sight of us at the same tine [sic] we could see a snow Storm amonge the mountain tops, this looked superbly grand on the 4 of July, but was not quite so pleasant to our feelings physically. White frost & ice last night[.][17] These Springs and surrounding scenery presents a degree of interest beauty and grandure that the combined Continents of the Whole World can't excel. We traveled say 23 miles to day Sunday as it was & the 4 of July too. This point is the extreme northern extent of Bear river. the river a mile or two from the Springs makes a turn around a very high precipitous mountain and takes a southern direction;[18] at this point we bid farewell to old Bear river and that without any regrets not with standing the valley of this river presents better soil & more variety of scenery than any region of the same extent, that we have yet passed. This 4th of July will be ever remembered

## JULY 1 - JULY 31, 1852

by me as connected with a train of interest awakened by the rarity grandure and variety of scenery & all else connected with or calculated to arouse genuine thought. Here I enjoyed my self!!!!

---

[11] The name, from Platt and Slater, *Travelers' Guide*, p. 16, does not appear on modern maps. Turnbull also refers to it as "Ashes or Ashlies" creek (*Travels from the United States*, p. 185). Possibly it is either Threemile Creek or Georgetown Creek, both intermittent streams.

[12] North Hill above Georgetown, Idaho.

[13] Soda Springs, Idaho. See below, note 16. Trappers referred to the springs as Beer Springs.

[14] A hand-drawn map in John Lewis's manuscript "Diary," p. 97, places a trading post on the west side of a creek, which he names Spring Creek (now Soda Creek), near its junction with Bear River.

[15] Turnbull describes ". . . a Snake Village all built with wigwams covered by Buffaloe skins one Log House a Northwest trader or traders French & Americans, every thing mostly for sale Ponies in 100s all colours & kinds pretty near as good as the Montreal Ponies Blacksmiths shop, Indians here to shew [shoe] their Hunters here [*sic*], it is a handsome place . . ." (*op. cit.*, p. 185). Mrs. Francis Sawyer said: "We see lots of Indians now, and some are at our camp most all the time. They usually want to trade fish for fish hooks and something to eat" (*op. cit.*, p. 11).

[16] All diarists give detailed descriptions of the springs. See, for example, Silas V. Miller, "Letter to his brother, Nov. 24, 1852," pp. 12–14. Frémont also described them at length; see *Report of the Exploring Expedition*, pp. 135-139.

Emigrants found the effervescent water of some of the springs quite palatable. Mrs. Sawyer, for example, ". . . made some soda drinks and cream tartar with the water, and they were nice and cool" (*op. cit.*, p. 11). Most springs are covered today by Soda Point Reservoir, formed by a dam on Bear River.

[17] The Sawyer party was at Soda Springs on July 4, the same day Wayman was also there. "It is quite cool here this evening," Mrs. Sawyer wrote, "and it snowed in the mountain[s] and rained in the valley where we were" (*op. cit.*, p. 11). The next day: "We found ice on the water in camp this morning, so you can see how cold it sometimes is here on the glorious Fourth. We were glad to get the ice water to drink" (*ibid.*, p. 11).

[18] Bear River turns abruptly south around what was once called Sheep Rock, now known as Soda Point. After flowing through Idaho and northern Utah, it empties into Great Salt Lake.

**JULY 5th Monday, 1852** Hooked up tolerably late this morning and bid farewell to the Mineral Springs and old Bear river[.] our road lay over a level valley for some 18 miles in a western direction, after which we assended a long sloping ravine between two mountain ranges, gained the summit and desended into a hollow.[19] Where we are encamped for the night Grass Wood & Water plenty and good. We have passed over 21 miles to day. Nothing of unusual interest occurring to day, I will close my story and Eat Supper[.]

One hour later. I this morning baught a fine Buffaloe robe of an old Indian for which I paid five dollars and a check shirt; This will come in good play as the nights are very cold here; — Cold enough for frost every night[.] About two miles south of our road opposite to the Fort Hall road to the left[20] was an old Crater the top of which is 100 feet from the level, the mouth some 300 feet in diameter and 75 feet deep with an abundance of Scoria & Lava scattered in all directions.[21] The Mountains here are made up of Trap Basalt & Syenite[.]

[19] They moved west close to where U.S. 30N and State Highway 34 run today, past Alexander (a station on the Union Pacific R.R.), and on toward Lund, Idaho. From here the trail moved southwesterly and upward over a pass in the Fish Creek Range. The hollow in which Wayman's party camped is near the head of Fish Creek and south of the gravel road which crosses the pass today.

The route they were following, which was recommended by Platt and Slater, was the Hudspeth-Myers cutoff, first opened in 1849 by Benomi M. Hudspeth and John J. Myers, who wanted a shorter way to the Humboldt River that would avoid the northern and, they thought erroneously, longer route via Fort Hall on the Snake River. See Dale E. Morgan, ed., *The Overland Diary of James A. Pritchard*, pp. 144n, 159–160n., and George R. Stewart, *The California Trail*, pp. 250–53. The trail is mapped in *Route of the Oregon Trail in Idaho* (Second printing, 1967).

[20] Wayman means that the Hudspeth cutoff was to the left. The road to Fort Hall, which was on the Snake River north of today's Pocatello, Idaho, bore to the right through Gem Valley toward the Portneuf River.

[21] Wayman's "old crater" is Alexander Crater. Actually there are three cinder cones, or remnants of them, in the area, although other diarists also mention only one. Esther B. Hanna said there was "... one mound standing near the junction of the roads" (*Canvas Caravans*, p. 67). She remarked at some length upon the lava-covered area, which today is dotted with farm buildings and is covered in summer with rich grain fields. One emigrant, Jay Green, found "... the crater of a volcano into which I did decend about twelve feet" ("Diary," p. 16).

**JULY 6th 1852 Tuesday**   A cloudy gloomy morning, yoked up the oxen up [*sic*] and left Mountain Willow Creek,[22] and bent our course westward over a long assent and through a mountain gorge into a small valley[23] where we found a Wigwam & Whiskey at a 25 a pop [?] or 1.50 per pint: This was situated on the Pannack river,[24] as I call it[,] some 5 or 6 miles from Mountain Willow Creek, We then Passed over some moderate assints [*sic*] and desents[25] and came to the river again after traveling some 3 miles[;] here we nooned. The mountains through this region are very bold & rugged – some snow capped & others clothed with Cedar in spots[.]

During the afternoon we assended a long slope[26] & desended into a broad valley called Marsh or Rush Valley, traveled up this valley some distance and came to crossed and camped on the west bank of Marsh Valley Creek, after passing over 17 miles.[27] Here I found some specimens of colored Quartz & Absinth'ea [*sic*] &c. This creek comes directly from the mountains & [is] made of melted snow. Grass & water plenty, but Wood scarce – Small Sage bushes. It rained a heavy shower this evening. And still remains cloudy and threatening. Very cold for July[,] this is[;] over coat on all day[.]

[22] The name in Platt and Slater for Fish Creek.

[23] Perhaps Wayman refers to the junction of Fish Creek and the Portneuf River, a short distance east of Lava Hot Springs; but it is more likely that he means a point somewhat farther west where Dempsey Creek flows into the Portneuf.

[24] The Bannock River lies far west of Wayman's present location. By *Pannack* he means the Portneuf River. None of these names appears in Platt and Slater; but Horn's *Overland Guide*, which Wayman or someone else in his party probably had, incorrectly identifies the Portneuf as a "Branch of Panack River" (p. 39). Wayman would have had no other reason for using this name.

[25] The trail wound through hills lying southwest of Lava Hot Springs.

[26] Five miles west of Lava Hot Springs, a gravel road closely approximating Wayman's route winds southwest over open and rolling cultivated hills toward Arimo, Idaho.

[27] "Valley Marsh Creek" appears in Platt and Slater, p. 17. Marsh Creek, which runs north roughly parallel to U.S. 191, flows into the Portneuf River. Thus, in traveling up the valley, Wayman's party was moving south, using a detour from the regular route. They camped somewhere south of Arimo.

24[28]

**Wednesday JULY 7th 1852**  Well this was a tolerably fair morning. We made an early starte & drove over a moderately long assent though not as bad as usual and came to Willow Creek after driving 12 miles & nooned, — after which we took up our line of march & made a drive of some 11 or 12 miles over an excellent road laying along a desending hollow between two Mountains the most of the way, & arrived at Gravel Creek where we are encamped for the night.[29] Good Grass, Water & Sage wood. Baught 1 bushel of potatoes for $3.00[.]

[28] From now on, Wayman frequently writes at the top of a page the number of miles traveled that day.

[29] Their route this day took them west over the divide between Marsh Creek and the watershed of the Malad River, which flows south. Willow Creek (Willow Muddy Creek in Platt and Slater, p. 17) is Dairy Creek, an affluent of the Little Malad. Moving south, they came to the Little Malad (Gravel Creek?) and camped near the outlet of Sublett Canyon. Of Gravel Creek, Platt and Slater wrote: "This is good water and full of trout. You now soon enter a ravine and gradually rise the mountain" (pp. 17–18).

24

**Thursday JULY 8th**  A fine white frost this morning, got a late starte, and commenced assending a very long norrow Gorge[30] between two mountains say from the Creek to summit 7 miles, thence to valley[31] 3[32] more miles, From the summit to foot of main mountain a mile or more the road lieing[33] in a deep winding ravine just room enough for a Wagon without the driver.[34] This reminds me of a portion of Holy Writ Where it speaks of the strait and norrow way. this place answered the description very well with the exception of a fiew short crook, & turns[.]

Took a short noon and drove over a very long assinding [*sic*] Moun[tain] & across a valley, distance 10 miles thence down a gradual desent 4 miles and found a Spring by the road side where we encamped for the night.[35] Here I found a man dying with the Cholera[.] Wood very scarce, grass good some mile or more from Camp. The Mountains here are all bare and smoothe. It is awful dusty these times. By Ging it beats everything in the dust line[.] Traveled in all to day 24 miles. Cold nights yet, yes very cold[.]

---

[30] Sublett Canyon.

[31] Arbon Valley, through which flows Deep Creek.

[32] *Or* is crossed out after *3*.

[33] *Lieing* is written over *laying*.

[34] Platt and Slater wrote that from the summit "You now descend through a deep and difficult ravine" (p. 18). The difference in elevation is approximately 600 feet.

[35] They had crossed the southern end of the Deep Creek Mountains and descended into Rockland Valley, through which flows the south fork of Rock Creek. The spring to which Wayman refers is probably the one that appears on modern maps as Big Rock Spring, although about two miles east is Twin Springs and two miles south is Quaking Asp Spring. See Irene Paden, *The Wake of the Prairie Schooner*, pp. 315–16.

20

**Friday JULY 9th 1852** A late starte again, made a drive of some twenty miles to day all told, through a very uneaven region, the assents to day were not difficult but very long through Mountain Ravines sometimes very stony & hard on the cattle's feet. We this evening found Muddy Creek & traveled down its valley some three miles and stoped for the night[.][36] Mountains here bold high and ruggid though destitute of timber.— Some Aspen groves occasionally along the branches. This was an unusually fine pleasant day[.]

---

[36] From Big Rock Springs, Wayman's party had angled northwest into the Summit Range, passed Summit Spring (Platt and Slater, p. 18), and descended into the east side of Raft River valley along Sublett Creek, which Wayman, following Platt and Slater (p. 18), calls Muddy Creek. For the identity of the two streams, see Paden, p. 319.

23

**Saturday JULY 10th** Left our encampment this morning early, and bent our course south west, (after crossing the East baranch [*sic*] of Raft River) Across Raft River valley.—[37] This valley is some twenty miles wide — while it looks to [be] not more the [than] 5 miles[.] This evening finds us encamped upon the West and main fork of Raft River after traveling over 23 miles[.] some six

# JULY 1 - JULY 31, 1852

miles before reaching the West fork we crossed two very muddy branches near together. Wood grass & Water plenty and of good quality[.] This Valley is one of the most beautiful and (pleasant)[38] *fine* vallies that I have yet seen. To the right in a north western direction you can see the sharp peaks of towering mountains capped with eternal snow — hundreds of miles in the distance — this a most magnificent view. These Raft River mountains in our immediate vicinity are lofty and grand, being capped with snow. While it is quite warm in the valley during the day — were it not for a strong b[r]eeze occasionally (which is quite cool) it would be oppressively hot[.] Clear & dry to day, and dusty, dusty, dusty.

---

[37] Raft River, which flows north into the Snake River, was the route which emigrants followed who had taken the road to Fort Hall. The Hudspeth cutoff and the Fort Hall route merged southeast of Malta, Idaho, on Cassia Creek, which Wayman refers to below as "the West and main fork of Raft River." Platt and Slater warned that "This stream is difficult to cross, being deep and muddy" (p. 19).

[38] *Pleasant,* enclosed in parentheses in the manuscript, is written over one or more illegible words.

**Sunday JULY 11th 1852** We are remaining in camp to day, and keeping the Lord's day as well as we conveniently can. Last night was cloudy and warm for this region, the warmest night since we struck the Mountains. This morning found it raining moderately which was kept up during the whole fore noon. I was called to see Mr[.] Egleston Very low with Colleguitru [?] Diarrhea approaching very nearly Genuine [?] Cholera. he is some better this morning and may yet live with care though very doubtful. I was called on the night of the 8 to see a man dying of Cholera from north end name Joseph Peck[.] A very fine warm afternoon — A Very fine pot of bean soupe for dinner — I am devoting my servises to necessary business while some are card playing — others lounging, some Cooking, and some looking on, while I am very sorry to say our Minister seems disposed to spend the day triming heads, some bad heads too yes very bad ones, I might say with propriety rascally ones. If he would first convert the reprobates, then he would be excuseable, but as it is I know not where he expects pardon for Heaven denies him[.]

27

**Monday JULY 12th** Made a very early start & drove over a very firm & good road some 27 miles and encamped in Granite City one of the finest Natural places of its kind in the World,[39] I banter the World to beat it[.] This City is Walled in on every side with towering Granite mountains some peaks shooting athwart the sky like towering domes. While hundreds of piles, peaks, steeples & domes of all shapes posible in the distance looking like an old delapidated City. In a south Eastern direction may be seen a large mountain made up of Mica schist[.] This after noon we passed through a most beautiful basin surrounded with fine

Mountains. To this Granite City seems to be but two out lets, a narrow gorge where we entered, and a wider space where we made our exite[.] Here I obtained several specimens[,] one from the Mansion house as I call it, as a token of remembrance[.] This City is situated near the half way place between Raft River and Goose Creek[.] The weather is and has been much milder for two days than usual for this part of God's Creation[.] Grass, Wood and Water good & plenty[.]

---

[39] Their route had taken them up Cassia Creek to where Alba, Idaho, is located today. Moving in a generally southwest course which took them over several small tributaries of Raft River, they reached a point about where Almo, Idaho, is located and then entered a narrow gorge through which flows Circle Creek (a gravel road today follows an almost identical route). Wayman's Granite City was more commonly known in the mid-nineteenth century as City of Rocks, although it bore other names as well: "City of Castles" (Bruff, *Gold Rush*, p. 116); "Steeple Rocks" (J. M. Daughters, "Journal," p. 137); "Pyramid Circle" (Alpheus Graham, "Journal," p. 16, and Horn's *Overland Guide*, p. 44). The area is a pocket walled in by hills and mountains within which are large rock formations eroded into curious, monumental shapes. Alpheus Richardson described them by writing: "This is one of the most picturesque scenes on the route. Some of them are from 50 to 75 feet high with tops projecting over the sides similar to a house. Some are round with the top projecting all one way and are soft and can be cut with a knife. The emigrants have cut their names on the sides of some. Some of the names have been on several years, and some are so cut up that there is no more room for more names" ("Diary," pp. 15–16). See also Andrew Child, *Overland Route to California*, pp. 42–43; Eliza A. Egbert, whose "Diary," pp. 41–42, also contains a good description; and Elisha D. Perkins, *Gold Rush Diary*, p. 99.

**Tuesday JULY 13th** We this morning left Granite City and commenced our daily toil. drove to Mountain Spring Creek say a distance of 14 miles & nooned.[40] Some d–d Indians sneaking around beging.[41] As usual McT. & Loring were conjureing around the Squaws. I saw them give her (the Squaw) some victuals with a greateal [great deal] of care, & solicitude without receiving any thing in return in sight. they were seen going in the direction that the squaw indicated and return[ed] with out any explanation[.]

27

We left our nooning ground and started along — and traveled 13 miles Finding our selves in Goose Creek Valley where we are encamped for the night[.] Grass & Water good but Wood very scarce[.][42] I obtained a very fine specimen of Mica A little Quartz & Felspar — among the Goose Creek Mountains.

---

[40] They had come through Junction Valley and were crossing the Goose Creek Mountains by way of Granite Pass, southwest of Moulton, Idaho. Near the summit was Mountain Spring, which Platt and Slater left unnamed, although they wrote: "As you ascend the mountain you will find a good spring of water near the road on your right" (p. 20). ". . . The road leading up towards the Goose Creek mountains," Tosten K. Stabaek noted, "was hilly and

rocky, and pasture for the cattle was scarce. But there were some great springs along the road" (*An Account of a Journey to California in 1852*, p. 117).

[41] Numerous diarists report Indians frequenting this area. Mrs. Francis Sawyer, for example, wrote in her diary on July 14: "The Digger Indians stole thirteen mules and one ox, last night, from a company just ahead of us. We camp with some company every night now and keep a strong guard out all the time, for the Indians will steal the animals if they get half a chance" (*op. cit.*, p. 12).

[42] Although Platt and Slater call attention to the fact that the descent into Goose Creek valley was by way of "a very hilly road for several miles" (p. 20), Wayman ignores its difficulties. One 1849 traveler wrote: "Then the descents were frightful to look at[.] We rough locked them [the wagons] and pulled back on them with our ropes. . . . To look up at the waggons toward the top they looked as if they were on end" (Elijah B. Farnham, "From Ohio to California in 1849," quoted by John F. McDermott, ed., *An Artist on the Overland Trail*, p. 63n). Tosten Stabaek observed that here was ". . . a deep valley, with steep mountain sides, through which we reached the lower country. We had seen no fruit on our journey, but by Goose Creek there was an abundance of rather good-tasting berries" (*op. cit.*, p. 114).

24

**Wednesday JULY 14th** Well as usual we did start upon our Westward journey again — bending our course in a South Western direction up this Goose Creek Valley for near 20 miles — Where the Creek forks — the South branch coming down a deep ravine between two Mountains —[43] up this ravine we traveled 4 miles & camped for the night — on the south side of said ravine is a range of very steep Trap Mountains hundreds & hundreds of feet high arranged in a columnar form — This was most imposing and grand[.] Water plenty, but grass and wood scarce[.] Traveled 24 miles all told[.]

[43] "Leaving the head of the valley, you follow up the south fork through a cut in the mountain. Road not good" (Platt and Slater, p. 21).

18

**Thursday JULY 15th** This morning we left this Goose Creek branch assended some very rough stony slopes for some 7 miles after which the road was easy and pleasant — traveled 14 miles & nooned without wood grass or water — We were provided with water in our Canteens. This afternoon we traveled three miles and found good grass and water[.][44] here we stoped to graze the Cattle — and quite a hard thunder shower came up and lasted two hours or more[.] this decided us to remain in Camp during this afternoon and night — Here I found a fine specimen of Cornelian & Chalsedony [*sic*] this I have been looking to find since we struck the mountains but found none good till to day near this Thousand Spring Valley[45] where we are encamped for the night. The Mountains in this vicinity are comparatively small and even[.] The Humbolt Ms[.] can be seen in the south West. they look quite savage[.] We have probably traveled

71

18 miles to day. This rain will lay the dust and make it more agreeable traveling tomorrow. tomorrow we will find the boiling spring I expect.

---

[44] Thomas Turnbull, following the same route, said that ". . . after leaving the stream we ascended & descended a long hill which is almost entirely covered with small stones up & down the road crooked   no water & no grass for 16 miles   4 miles below spring good grass no water much   Creek pretty near dry   on entering this valley a little at the right under a ledge of Rock is a spring of good water though a little warm when first taken" (*Travels from the United States,* p. 190). Both Turnbull and Wayman were relying upon Platt and Slater, where they read: "On entering this valley, a little at the right, under a ledge of rocks, is a spring of good clear water, though a little warm when first taken out. It is called *Rock Spring*" (p. 21).

What this tells us is that Wayman's party, having traveled southwest up Goose Creek (in the northwest corner of Elko County, Nevada) had crossed over a divide and struck the source of Rock Springs Creek (as it is named today), which flows southwest into Thousand Springs Creek at Eccles Ranch. An unimproved road now follows the route of the old trail.
[45] Wayman found the name in Platt and Slater, p. 22. Emigrants usually referred to it as Hot Springs Valley, a term Wayman also uses in his next diary entry.

## 20

**Friday JULY 16th** A cloudy warm morning something unusual for this region. We traveled in a south West direction up the Hot Spring Valley 20 miles, and are encamped upon a low bluff near the south Western extremity of said Valley, grass good but no water or wood, this we can put up with for the sake of our Cows — This evening about 4 Oclock we came to the Hot Springs — numerous small Springs bulging from a Muddy Slough, of various temperatures. The hotest being about 120°[.] Within a fiew miles from this place we expect to find the boiling springs. This is a very fine Valley being some 4 or 5 miles at this point surroundid with fine even M.s. These hot springs are of the same Mineral character that the springs are on the Bear River, presenting the same incrustations where the water is quiet, of the same taste, though not so strong with Carbonic Acid Gass, while they are much hotter[.][46]

---

[46] That these springs were a great curiosity to emigrants is evident from entries in numerous diaries: "we saw springs of all varieties cold, sulphur, alkali, poison, and some so hot that a person could not put his hand in the water two minutes without being scalded   some [emigrants] washed their clothes in these springs. grass around was abundant" (John Verdenal, "Journal," p. 35); ". . . passed the Boiling Springs boiling like hot water on the fire full of Alkali" (Turnbull, p. 190); ". . . I find the boiling springs here are many springs — some so hot that I cannot bear my hand in them — steam arises — One of these springs make[s] a huming bubling nois . . ." (Jay Green, *Diary,* p. 17). Richard Hickman wrote that seventy yards above one hot spring was ". . . another excellent spring of cold water" (*An Overland Journey,* p. 16). Clouds of vapor rose from the warm springs, he noted, and the air had a bad odor. See also Mrs. Francis Sawyer, p. 13, and Platt & Slater, p. 22.

## 26

**Saturday JULY 17th** A fine morning, rained a very little this fore noon[.] our road to day was quite easy and good being along a valley all day — traveled 26 miles and encamped near a natural well & good grass[.][47] Sage Wood  To day found some specimens of Petrified Wood &c[.] The Humbolt M.s. look ruggid and bold, being capped with snow.[48] The M.s. along this valley are comparatively low and even[.] The earth here looks quite ashy and strongly Alkaline[.] Standing water not fit for use[.]

---

[47] Their most likely route would have been to follow Thousand Springs Creek to Brush Creek and then to Town Creek, which would lead them directly to some wells located about two miles north of present-day Wells, Nevada. Jay Green, who came this way wrote: "I travel over many hills   at length I come into a large valley and encamp   I find many wells . . ." (*Diary*, p. 17). These wells supply the city with water today.

[48] These mountains lie southwest of Wells, Nevada.

## 18

**The Lord's Day JULY 18th**  Well, being only a short distance from the Humbolt say 18 miles, we concluded to pay the said Humbolt a visit Sunday as it is. The road from this place was unexpectedly easy, we made the drive by 4 Oclock easy and are now in Camp for the night, & probably during tomorrow. We entered the main valley through a continuation of the Hot Spring Valley, the main Valley coming in with the river from the north on our right[.][49] Here, where we are encamped the valley is near 15 — or 20 miles wide and thickly set with fine grass[.][50] The Humbolt at this fork is quite small, not being more than 10 or 15 feet wide and 6 or 8 inches deep, though it is low at this time. The Mountains upon the East Side are Very high and ruggid spotted with snow[.] The water of the Humbolt is good enough, but it is too warm to be pleasant[.] No wood at all save some shrubby willow skirting the banks of the river.[51] No rain to day for variety sake[.] The sky looks clean and pure with a feiw white fleecy clouds floating slowly athwart the Heavens; the air is balmy & pleasant & all else right I think I do[.]

---

[49] It is not clear whether the "river from the north" is the East Fork of the Humbolt or Marys River, both of which come together at Deeth, Nevada, a point which corresponds to Wayman's mileage figure. Marys River flows from the north and the East Fork from the northeast.

[50] Verdenal points out that ". . . this year the river had risen in spring & overflowed the banks which caused the fine grass our cattle enjoyed to grow in abundance" ("Journal," p. 36).

[51] Because Indians sometimes lay concealed in them, the willows were a source of apprehension for emigrants. G. A. Smith, for example, remarked: "this Stream is the Travelers fear as the Indians are verry bad on it" ("Diary," June 23; no pagination).

**Monday JULY 19th**  We remained in port all day to recruit our teams, & sun & air our eatables. A very cold night last night was   ice & frost this morning though quite warm during the day. I visited the bluffs to day for a load of Sage, and found a good specimen of Chalcedony. This Valley is very spacious and picturesque — Grass heavy & fine —

All well & in fine spirits I mean Cattle horses & mules as well as the balance of us — Weather glorious and heartsom — roads splendid & all things right[.]

25

**Tuesday JULY 20th** Quite a cool morning this was — We rigged up our teams and commenced our journey down the Humbolt Valley — After traveling 21 miles we came to & crossed the North fork of the said Humbolt; — after which we traveled 4 miles & camped for the night, after passing over 25 miles. After crossing the north fork we passed over two stony hills of moderate altitude; the road very good, but awful dusty. The Ms. in the distance towering and bold snow capped as usual. Grass & water plenty[.] Willow & Sage for wood. A clear fine day this,

27

**Wednesday JULY 21st** We this good day traveled 27 miles and camped near the first ford[52] of the Humboldt at the end of the Valley — The road to day was dusty! dusty!! dusty!!![53] otherwise very good. The mountains in our immediate vicinity are comparatively low smoothe & even[.] yesterday evening I found some good specimens which I preserved[.] This is the warmest day that has been out since the year 1852 commenced — the nights are yet quite cool — mornings and evenings very pleasant, just cool enough to make you feel fine[.]

---

[52] This may be the Indian ford to which Platt and Slater refer on p. 23.

[53] A. M. Crane also complained of the dust: ". . . [it] has been very bad, rising in clouds so thick, as to almost suffocate both men & cattle." On successive days he wrote: "dust almost suffocating," "dust intolerable" ("Journal," pp. 65-70). Some emigrants who had thought to bring goggles used them to keep the dust out of their eyes (John M. Verdenal, "Journal," p. 23).

18

**Thursday JULY 22nd** A beautiful fine clear cool and very pleasant morning — After Tater [sic] we hooked up our stock and again commenced *the said* tour westward, and after traveling some 15 miles came to and nooned on Cold Spring Creek: Here we Tatered again and drove say 3 miles and concluded to put up till morning in Consequence of a stretch of 18 or 20 miles without grass commencing at this point. Our animals concluded that it would be no good place to tabernicle[54] [sic] amonge the M.s. with out grass. So we will stay here[.] We crossed the river 4 times within 10 miles travel[.] The river here winds its way through a deep ravine and very high mountains on both sides composed of Conglomerate, Trachyte Trap and Basalt intermingled in all varieties[.]

# JULY 1 - JULY 31, 1852

[54] Tabernacle. As an intransitive verb, it means "to reside temporarily" (*Webster's New International Dictionary*, 2nd ed.); thus in this context, to rest.

### 24

**Friday JULY 23rd** This morning we commenced our Mountain journay the 18 or 20 mile stretch and traveled on untill say near 2 Oclock and reached & crossed the river. While passing over the mountain I found some more specimens of Chalcedony and Agate. In all to day we have traveled say 24 miles all told — Bill Loring caught up with us this evening  all well  Grass and Wood scarce water plenty in the Humboldt, but too warm to be pleasant  Ms close around, low & even, but in the distance very high & ruff[.]

### 25

**Saturday JULY 24th** This day we went Kiting down the Humboldt Valley like Hell. After traveling some 11 miles we came to & crossed two points or spurs nearing the river so closely that we were forced to clime the Mountain. The Valley here is from 5 to 8 miles wide, covered generally with good grass[.] We have traveled in all to day 25 miles[.] Grass fine  Willow for wood and Humboldt water to drink[.] The whole Valley to day seemes to be covered with lava of the dark variety all well right right!!

### 25

**Sunday JULY 25th** A warm pleasant morning, some clouds floating leasurely through the Heavens, promising rain, but I fear this promise will not be redeemed — It is so very, very dusty & warm, that rain would be quite acceptable & refreshning [*sic*] — The M.s. are quite high and precipitous composed mostly of Trachitic rock. We are encamped on a Slough after traveling 25 miles[.] Grass good — Wood & water bad enough  A very fine balmy evening, the wind very pleasant, while the sun is seting beautifully, all right in our camp[.]

### 23

**Monday JULY 26th** Quite a warm and sultry to day — and the deepest — the finest — and most disagreeable dust that I ever saw[.] We drove say 15 miles and nooned upon the south side of the Humboldt river — This afternoon we hooked up and journied about 9 miles & encamped on the river bank for the night traveling over 23 miles in all — The Indians hooked a poney from a wagon in our train[;] some 6 or 9[55] men remained to hunt it out.[56] they found one Indian in the Willows and after shooting at him 4 times they succeeded in captureing the said Indian without any damage to either the Indian or themselves, — brave fellows I think — About 10 Oclock this evening our warriors came in Camp

75

with an Indian poney which they bravely succeeded in arresting from an Indian who happened to fall in their way during the time that the war fever was stimulating them. This act of bravery and manliness should be recorded for the benefit of themselves & posterity — From all that I can learn I think that they murdered the Indian that they had in custody. A shame

55 The numeral 6 is written over 5, and 9 is written over 6.

56 The theft of animals was a source of annoyance to emigrants along much of the Humboldt. Verdenal's concern appears in his diary entry for September 3: "the river was so thickly bordered by willows that it could not have surprised us much to seeing indians among them"[.] His company had ". . . heard rumors that indians had robbed a train on ahead of us." During the night of September 10, they lost two horses to Indians, and another company had lost five the night before. See his "Journal," pp. 36–38.

24

**Tuesday JULY 27th** Well as usual we did commence our daily toil in tolerably good time and journied over 24 miles and are now encamped again upon the south side of said Humboldt[.] grass good Willow wood & Humboldt water[.] The river is here about the width of White water at Cambridge,[57] but affording ⅓ more water.

The mountains are very high and bold some snow in sight yet — The valley here is 8 or 10 miles wide. No timber save the Wild Sage and the Willows that skirt the river[.] We crossed a M. [mountain] to day composed intirely of H. Slate, T Slate & Quartz rocks[.]

57 The Whitewater River, a tributary of the Ohio River, flows south through Cambridge City, Indiana.

19

**Wednesday JULY 28th** A very warm day — traveled in all to day 19 miles and camped near the river. Grass good Willow Wood & Humboldt Water[.] The valley to day has been cut up with Sloughs and Willow bushes more than usual[.] These are very warm, yes very hot during the day — oppressively so. While the nights are quite warm until near day — when it is generally cool enough for comfort — I am quite tired of this Humboldt river — yes I want badly to find the end of said river — This is very disagreeable journeying[.][58]

58 Yet Caroline Richardson could exclaim at one point along the river: ". . . gained the summit a very sightly place as well as beautiful . . . the humbolt with its windings is all a sublime piece of scenery" ("Journal," p. 154). Few emigrants shared her reaction.

22

**Thursday JULY 9th** A warm morning. after driving some five miles we came to & crossed a sand bench of land say 3 miles wide very heavy rolling — & after journeying some 12 or 13 miles nooned among some low willows — This afternoon we hooked up and wagged over 10 miles & camped near the river in sight of a Trading post near a ford. Very cloudy & windy looking much like rain this evening. I hope it will[;] it would be fine for health & comfort[.] all else right[.]

24

**Friday JULY 30th** This morning we hooked up and crossed the river opposite a Trading post on the north side of the said Humboldt river and traveled about 12 miles and baited[59] upon the banks of the "R"[.]

This after noon we made a drive of some 12 miles & are now encamped near the river good grass Good Humboldt water and good Willow bushes for wood. Good Grub & Good health in our train all forked end down — Snow in sight in one place to day Ms high[.]

[59] That is, fed their animals.

24

**Saturday JULY 31st** Quite a warm day, the forenoon's drive was over a very good road; We baited near the river with out any grass or wood — passed on and soon commenced winding around amonge sand and clay banks, hollows, gutters, and ravines — not very hard, but awful dusty finally. Came to the river: — grass poor — Sage good. Mountains on the south side are very high & rocky[.] The valley here is very norrow & crooked with bluff clay & sandbanks — From this point we will take to the bench land again. A shower of rain last night. *(good)*

# August 1 – August 31, 1852

30

**Sunday AUGUST 1st**  A fine warm day. we drove till noon and remained in Camp until 3 oclock in the after noon — hooked up & drove till 12 at night — reaching the Meadows — Whose thousands of acres of grass are Seemingly designed for emigrants preparatory to comminc[i]ng [*sic*] the Desert which is 20 miles from this point — From where we are this valley looks to be hem[m]ed in in every direction with Ms. making one vast basin, as beautiful in apearance as it is gigantic in Size[.][1]

---

[1] In approximately this area, Caroline Richardson complained that the camp was ". . . a filthy place  this is a general camping ground and is well covered with skeletons from the first migration to the present . . . rendering the air very unhealthy  teams kept pouring in nearly all night . . ." ("Journal," p. 162, under date of August 27).

4

**Monday AUG 2nd**  We this morning hooked up and drove some 3 or 4 miles & came to [a] Trading post opposite the falls of the Humboldt. We neared the river & Camped for the day while we cut our grass for the Desert.[2] Grass fine water Good for this region, but wood miserably poor "Greece Wood" d–d mean[.] The M.s. in every direction are towering and grand while the valley looks like one vast ocean or Lake[.] I could take greate pleasure in contemplating this scenery wer[e] it not that I am sick & tired of this said Humbold[t.] I want to get out of this soon[.]

---

[2] Platt and Slater advised: "Here cut your grass for the desert" (*Travelers' Guide*, p. 26). Horn's *Overland Guide* stated: "Here is the beginning of the sink of the Humboldt River; the grass is to the left of the road, and is very plenty" (p. 53). Mrs. Francis Sawyer wrote that her party "cut some splendid grass" here on August 1 ("Overland to California," p. 15).

78

# AUGUST 1 – AUGUST 31, 1852

20

**Tuesday AUG 3rd** This was a very warm day, until near night, say 3 or 4 oclock it clouded up & the wind rose making quite comfortable. We made a drive of 20 miles to day, passing the sink, and Camping over a low bluff upon the bank of a Slough Coming from the South West — quite close to two Trading posts. We here spent the night preparatory to cr[o]ssing the c[e]lebrated Desert which commences at this point[.][3] The sink presents a very pretty appearance being several miles in width, quite a large sheet of water. M.s. in sight, some high, & others red[.] Quite Picturesque this is[.][4]

---

[3] Wayman read in Platt and Slater: "No grass or good water for 39½ miles. Here you prepare for the desert and pass over a small ridge, to a valley where a part of the water of Mary's river, having escaped from the lake, sinks" (p. 27). When John Verdenal arrived at this point on September 19, he found ". . . about five hundred wagons . . . recruiting their cattle to cross the dessert [*sic*]; and were cutting enormous masses of grass . . ." ("Journal," p. 40). His party also carried water from here in cans and barrels.

[4] When Caroline Richardson arrived, she observed that the lake, which was "of a bluish cast and looks smoky," was ". . . covered with myriads of large birds which resemble wild ducks[;] to night the air was fairly blackened with them[;] they are considered good eating" ("Journal," p. 165).

40

**Wendnsday AUG 4th** This morning we hooked up about 8 oclock and commenced the Desert journey, traveling till 1 Oclock making 16 miles & nooned. Where we now are baiting I can count 20 old dry carcasses.[5] This fills the bille for a Desert I believe. We commenced after resting 2 hours our Desert journey — we traveled until drak [dark] and ba[i]ted, after which we made the best of our way over the sand which was very heavy and deep. We passed 10 Trading Posts in traveling from The Humboldt sink to the Carson river[.][6] We struck the river about 40 miles above the sink — the river here is about 100 yards wide affording as much water as the Humboldt[.] This Desert is thickly studed with little mounds from 1 to 8 feet high & from 3 to 30 feet in diameter upon which a spicies of Greecewood grows — the rootss of which seem to hold the Mounds in shape. In other places the surface of the ground is perfectly smoothe & level, in the distance it looks like a sheet of water & reflecting the image of objects like a Miror[.][7] we traveled to day and last night 40 miles finding the river near sun up[.]

---

[5] This waterless stretch severely taxed the stamina of animals; and dead oxen, horses, and mules meant abandonment of wagons and their contents. Five days after Wayman traveled here, Alpheus Graham reported that "Wagons, horses, cattle and every other thing a man needs on this trip are strewed over this desert. Not less than 20 wagons, 40 horses and 50 cattle to every mile of the desert. The cattle and horses are all dried up with the skin on. I counted

56 wagon tires . . . [in] 100 yards and 47 in 40 yards. In many places whole teams are laying together[,] some times horses with the harness on them yet. I stood on one sand hill and counted 200 dead animals. But we did not see more than 15 that had been left this year [1852]" ("Journal," p. 18). Most of the losses he attributed to 1850. Similar scenes make up entries in the diaries of other emigrants. See, for example, Caroline Richardson, "Journal," p. 168; Mrs. Sawyer, "Overland to California," p. 16; and Verdenal, "Journal," p. 41.

[6] The Carson River rises in the Sierra Nevada Mountains south of Lake Tahoe and flows northeast until it drains into Carson Sink.

[7] Wayman here describes a mirage.

3

**Thursday AUG[8] 5th**  This morning just before sun up we arrived in Raggtown[9] upon the North bank of Carson river[.] we here watered the stock & drove 3 miles up the river and Camped for the day[.] The river banks affords some large Cotton Woods the finest that I have seen since I left the Missouri — the valley near the river affords some grass & numerous groves of Willow bushes — presenting rather an interesting scenery — a Grateful relief from the dull sameness of the barren past and Dreary Desert over which we have just traveled[.] Raggtown is well named, being made up of some 50 or more Pole and Canvass tents — Where can be found all kinds of vulgar amusements Whiskey & brandy of the worst possible quality for 25 cents per drink[.]

Bacon at 40 & 50 cts. per lb. flour at 25 cts. per lb[.] Grass generally eaten off, but some good grazing. Numerous trains are encamped along the bottom all resting from the fatigues of travel — many very many teams are left on the Desert[.]

[8] *Aug* is written over *July*.

[9] This settlement, which no longer exists, was located ". . . about 7 miles northwest of present Fallon [Nevada]. The trail across the desert ran about midway between the present line of the Southern Pacific Railroad and the modern road between Fallon and Lovelock" (Dale Morgan, ed., *Overland Diary of James A. Pritchard,* p. 167n.). The place was made up of shanties, tents, and brush huts. Supplies and food were available, with whisky in great demand. Thomas Turnbull said there were ". . . fellows from California Bakers Butchers Saloon traders of all kinds for the season Robert [?] has been here buying & selling Horses Waggons &c for 3 months so he said  5 or 6 of them make them a Wigwam & live like Indians[;] 100[s] of them follow the same  buy poor stock  cut grass &c feed them after they get a good many in the fall [they] drive them off to C-a [California]" (*Travels from the United States,* pp. 206–207). See also Lucy R. Cooke, *Crossing the Plains in 1852,* p. 68, and Caroline Richardson, "Journal," p. 169.

3

**Friday AUGUST[10] 6th**  We remained in Camp to day until 3 Oclock in the evening, hooked up & drove 3 miles and camped near the river. this is slow traveling

## AUGUST 1 - AUGUST 31, 1852

I think[.] Well this Carson Valley is a change from the tiersom sameness that that [*sic*] we have been subjected to for a long time[.] A shade tree is quite a luxury. I feel as though we were at home, & yet I am very anxious to be traveling[.] Tomorrow we will commence again in earnest & will soon meet any other change & what change remains yet to be seen[.]

[10] *August* is written over *July*.

### 16

**Saturday AUG**[11] **7th** This morning we got a late starte and drove some 16 miles without bating and are now encamped for the night upon the north bank of the Carson River. Grass moderately good, wood scarce through d—d foolery & Carson water to drink. This was quite a warm day, though a pleasant wind astur this evening. We are encamped near Two Trading posts where can be bought Whiskey, Brandy, Pies and other ketch penny fixens[.] Rather a rough stony road to day, all ilse [*sic*] right[.]

[11] *Aug* is written over *July*.

### 21

**Sunday AUG**[12] **8[th]** This good Lord's day we drove 21 miles and are encamped upon the north bank of Carson River, where we have fine grass good wood & Carson water[.] all to gether this is rather a treat, it not being often that we get those three articles at the same place[.] This forenoon we had 10 miles of deep sand & nooned, after which our road was quite good — This has been a splendid day, a cool breeze stiring all day[.] This evening we hove in sight of the S. Nevada M.s. snow capped they are. here we are "row, row[.]"

[12] *Aug* is written over *July*.

### 16

**Monday AUG**[13] **9th** A cool night last night was, and this morning is clear cool and very pleasant. We made a start and drove in all to day say 16 miles and are now encamped near a ten mile Desert which prevents us from pr[o]ceeding any further to day.[14] The M.s. on both sides of the river are very bold and picturesque, the intervening valley is from 3 to five miles wide[.] the Ms here are comp[o]sed of Basaltic & Trachitic rocks[.] These things are all fine of their kind. I am injoying it *quite well* &c &c[.]

[13] Again Wayman wrote *Aug* over *July*. Obviously he had no eraser.

[14] Their camp was near what is now Carson City, Nevada. Here Wayman later set himself up in practice as a physician.

# A DOCTOR ON THE CALIFORNIA TRAIL

15 — returned

**Tuesday AUG 10th** This morning I received a summons to visit Mr. LaFountain[15] & a Lady some 15 miles back, which I ob[l]iged, while the team went on to the main valley. From Raggtown up to the broad valley is often very norrow just room for the river without the road. Varying from this to some three miles or more in width[.] Very high Ms on both sides, & some ahead are white with snow — Nights cold in the after part and days warm until late in the Evening[.]

---

[15] LaFountain was in a company which included Rachel C. Bruce, whose diary refers to his illness as well as to Wayman's treating him. Under the dates of August 5 and 6, she wrote: "left Lafountain this morning on account of sickness. Fryday 6[.] Today laid over a waiting for Lafountain to come up with us" ("Diary," no pagination).

16

**Wednesday AUG 11th** This day I traveled 16 miles & camped with Mr. La Fountain & Co.[16] Well I rested rather poorly last night, not being quite warm enough for Comfort, and besides being grunting[?] my self. This was a fine day all things considered. Scores of Emigrants seek the first opportunity to sell their teems and pack over the M.s.[17] I would like to do so my self, but prices do not suit me. Times[?][18] go off very well   all things in the Hole[.]

---

[16] On Saturday, August 7, Rachel Bruce wrote in her diary: "the Doctor came and staid with us to night." The discrepancies in dates are explainable only on the grounds that either Wayman or Miss Bruce had made an error some time previously in day-to-day chronology, which could easily result from an absence of calendars. The error appears to be Miss Bruce's.

[17] The Sierra Nevada Mountains.

[18] Illegible word.

20

**Thursday AUG 12** This morning I left Mr. La Fountain and passed over about 20 miles and found the boys in Camp[19] doing very well, having made up their minds to remain here some 8 or 10 days, & wate the arrival of Bill Loring's team[;] if they do so I think that I will kite over the M — with some one else. It does not quite suit me to stop at this time[.] The Valley here widens out 10 miles and fine grass, lots of pine on the M.s. & M[ountain] water good, good, good[.]

---

[19] Their camp was on the Carson River approximately five miles northeast of Genoa, Nevada.

**Friday AUG 13th** This was a fine day, I rode down to the Mormon Station[20] about 5 miles from where we are encamped[.] Made a prescription & settled

82

with M La Fountain, came back, eat dinner and am now lounging on my Buffaloe in the Shade, wating for an opportunity to make a push over the M.s. The boys are wanting to remain here a fiew days[21] and I am quite willing that they should do so — A very fine breeze this evening making it very pleasant. I am some anxious to be traveling[.]

---

[20] Mormon Station is today the picturesque little community of Genoa, situated at the base of the Sierra Nevada about twelve miles south of Carson City. It was established in 1849 or 1850. Most emigrants using the Carson Pass route to California stopped here. They found an abundance of good water, grass, and fresh vegetables, especially turnips and potatoes. Mary S. Bailey described it by writing: ". . . it is truly a romantic spot saw a Post Office blacksmith shop and even heard the sound of the breakfast bell for the first time since we left St Joseph . . . most beautifully clear streams of water[.] Soil very rich . . ." ("Journal," p. 26). See also Jay Green, *Diary*, p. 19; Turnbull, *Travels from the United States*, p. 212; Mrs. F. Sawyer, "Overland to California," p. 17; Caroline Richardson, "Journal," p. 175; and A. M. Crane, "Journal," p. 73. Crane reported that a barrel of flour cost $50. See also Kelly, *First Directory of Nevada Territory*, pp. 54–55. Genoa, he says, was ". . . the earliest settled, and for a long time the only town in Western Utah . . ." (p. 54).

[21] Platt and Slater advised ". . . all to stop in this valley and recruit their teams before crossing the Nevada mountains" (p. 28). The most difficult terrain of the entire journey lay ahead.

**Saturday AUG 14th** Well I lay around the Tent all day to day and shit gormanized and grunted,— I am d—d tired of this arrangement and will chop it off soon as possible. I consider this as being the hight of d—d foolery to remain here to no other purpose than annoying myself to no good purpose. The days are very hot from 10 in the morning till 3 in the evening when a brisk breeze rises and keeps up until night making it quite pleasant[.] Nights calm and serene[.]

**Sunday AUG 15th** In Camp all day, very warm about noon, afternoon very windy as usual — Not many[22] to day. The atmosphere look[s] smoky & portend[s] rain. The Ms in the West are clothed with a luxurunt growth of pine which contrasts strongly with the base appearance of those in the south East which are destitute of any timber[.] The Valley at this point may be 15 or 20 miles in width intersected with Sloughs & covered with grass[.]

---

[22] One illegible word appears after *many*.

---

**Monday AUG 16th** Well we are lounging around here to no purpose only to gratify some d—d fools who are not prepared to appreciate any kindness[.] The day was fine as usual, in the afternoon went out to the Ms hunting killed nix. The Range on the North West side of Valley are made of Granite, Syenite and Gneiss rocks. The soil in the Valley is composed of the detritis of the above named rocks. The ground glitters with it. I feel dogged in consequince of this detention. *"Hell"*

**Tuesday AUGUST 17th** This was a fine pleasant morning after brakefast I & B Loring went to the Mormon Station, I to see some sick ones & Bill to get a game, we both succeeded very well[.] we returned at noon & partook bountifully of some Sage Hen Soupe[.] Between our Ranch & the M. Station, around a spurr of Ms for a half mile or more, are numerous springs[;] in deed the [water] seemes to come out all along as warm as 100° or warmer[.]

This water is impregnated with Sulp[h]ate of Iron Lime & Carbonic aced gass[.] We see daily, numerous Traders from California mostly hard cases, though I occasionally find a human[?] man[.] The M.s. on our right are well clothed with Pine some 3 feet in diameter or more from this size down to the bush[.] These Ms are very steep abrupt and cone shaped yes and very high, — high enough to hold Eternal snow — this does pretty will [well] I think while it is hot August weather in the Valley where we are. Numerous Sloughs run in various directions over this valley, their course indicated by the Willows[.]

**Wednesday AUG 18th** Went this morning again to the Station and returned by noon. Col. Bentley overtook us this day, all right — This day is as all days have been since we Came here, fine and nice as you colud [could] ask. Time draggs slowly away and will so long as we stay here inactive[.] Tomorrow I am in hopes that we will make a start once more and put the thing through and be done with it so mote it be[.]

**Thursday AUG 19th** I am here yet annoyed like Hell in consequence of this infernal delay[.] This day is in all respects just like all other days — I visited the Station to day again and I hope to God for the last time, at least for the present. Again I indulge the hope that we will succeed in the effort[.] Windy this after noon as usual.

The Game of this Valley is principally Sage Hens upon which we live finely[.] this does pritty well[.]

**Friday AUG 20th** Shit, Hell, and Granny with a cock & ballocks[.] Damnation and Hellfier Camphire Forx [Fox?] Fier and all else that is mean, low and shitting. May the Good Lord ever deliver me from such Asses for all Coming time, and I will thank him Kindly, and return the Compliment the first practical apportunity [*sic*][.]

**Saturday AUG 21st** The same G d—d Hell fiered time[?] is going on as usual by the same "G—d—d" Fool. I am beaten to death when D—d Laziness and

G d d foolery are Trumps[.] Hell is full of such creatures and I have no doubt but much more worthey ones. I don't know and I hope never to know any more than I now do if I must learn by experience[.] save! Lord save!! else I perish[.]

16

**Sunday AUG 22nd**  Well, through Mercy we have started and traveled in all to day 16 miles and are encamped in the Mouth of the Canōn [sic][.][23] If some Evil Spirit does not again interfere we will resume our jaunt tomorrow & try the realities of a full Grown Mountain[.] This has been one very fine pleasant day — and full of interest on account of our good fortune in making a new start with our "*Eye Sore*"[.] To Hell! with all such.

---

[23] The canyon of the West Fork of Carson River leading to Carson Pass across the Sierra Nevada. The Carson Pass route, as George Stewart points out, continued after 1848 to be the principal road into California from the east (*The California Trail*, p. 206). Stewart discusses its advantages over the Truckee River route on p. 207.

16

**Monday AUG 23rd**  Well we commenced the said Canōn road and we found it to fill the bill entirely, notwithstanding the worst road that ever was traveled[.][24] We made 10 miles and are now encamped for noon upon Pine Creek[.][25] Hooked up and made a drive of about 6 miles & Encamped for the night — Pine wood very plenty and Water good, though the grass is scarce[.] Yellow and Spruce Pine in abundance[.] The Mountains are of the boldest character, very high and precepitous and Composed almost entirely of Granite rock[.] Indeed from Carson Valley to the present point I have seen but little else than the Granite in connection with Syenite. At the head of Carson Valley I saw some Syenitic Porphyry for the first time in my life.

Syenitic Porphyry[,] Syenite[,] amd Granite are all or very nearly all that you will see from Carson Valley up to the sumit of the first ridge[.] What is on hand further along still remains to be seen, though I will note it down as it presents its self[.]

Now while I am writing I look around me and and [sic] see precipitous Mountains in every direction with an abundance of snow and a full grown Wilderness of Pines. This looks Grand and awful, yet I believe that I enjoy it as well or better than any one now on the road. True I am annoyed beyond measure, but I beare it manfully knowing that my deliverance is close at hand, after which I will be prepared to use this richly earned lesson for all Coming time to my *own advantage*[.]

---

[24] Platt and Slater, p. 29, warned travelers of the extreme difficulty of this route, which is followed closely today by Highway 88. Some diarists found words inadequate to describe

its obstacles, while others left a good idea of what these were. Thomas Turnbull, for example, wrote: "it surpasses all i ever saw for large rock  hardly wide enough for a Waggon & rocks tons weight to scramble over half the height of a waggon  no track for the wheels or horses, but just enough to roll up & down the best way they can" (*Travels from the United States,* p. 214). Some emigrants abandoned wagons and carriages altogether; others carried them over the rocks. "Such a canyon never was seen before," wrote Mary Bailey; "the scenery was delightful but the roads dreadful —" ("Journal," p. 26).

Although Wayman does not mention them, three bridges crossed the river within a distance of four miles (Platt and Slater, p. 29).

25 This name does not appear in Platt and Slater nor on modern topographical maps.

18

**Tuesday AUG 24th** This day we saw and passed over the two sumits of the S. *Nevada* M.s. and of all d—d places that mortal beings ever saw or passed with teams this is the d—d—st[.][26] Well we got over safely & are now encamped upon a back bone of a M. just this side of the Main Sumit some 4 miles distant[.] It is quite airy up here —

Grass very scarce & a long ways to it[.] we had to take the Cattle one long mile down the M along a norrow ravine[.] 18 miles

26 Wayman fails to mention Red Lake, which the trail skirted along its south side. At its head was a very steep incline: "then we commenced what I Call ascending," wrote Thomas Turnbull; "terrible to look up  to ever conceive how a team could ever Scramble up  straight up  crooked & all shapes amongst the lofty pines & Rocks . . ." (p. 215). To John Verdenal, also, "It was very steep & encumbered with immense rocks, we had to take up wagon, by wagon, we hitched 10 yoke of oxen on each wagon, never had we been in worse passages" ("Journal," p. 44). Caroline Richardson looked at it as "a place too bad to think of." Her company came to a steep, smooth rock, and ". . . before we were aware of it the horses could not find footing and all stumbled together  our wagon commenced a retreat  using rocks blocks or lock chains we succeeded in cramping the wagons and stopped long enough to rest and take of [off] the lead horses and led them over rock and by means of ropes at the end of the tongue got over safe over steep pitches and gained the top  here took off our horses and went back to help the rest of our co[mpany]  all reached the top in safety" ("Journal," pp. 181–182).

From the high rim above Red Lake, one can only marvel that these people were able to make this terribly difficult ascent. Beyond lay a second summit, which Platt and Slater informed their readers was at 9000 feet above sea level: "You have now passed over 24¼ [of] the longest miles ever measured with wheels" (p. 30). After making the long climb, Mary Bailey, contemplating the snow and chill in the air and the desolation of a strange land, voiced her feelings by writing: ". . . how I wish we had a house to live in now:— If it were not for hope the heart would break" ("Journal," p. 27).

18

**Wednesday AUG 25[th]** This day we hooked up & found our way to Leek Springs[27] after traveling about 16 miles over a bad road. Here we drove our stock 1½ miles and found some grass. During the fore noon we found 5 miles of what may be called good road though the balance of the day made it all up again[.] Cedar 6 feet or more in diameter & Fir & Pine from 1 to 10 feet in diameter[.] And all the varieties that belong to the pine tribe[.]

---

[27] So named because of the onion-like leek plants growing here. Readers of Platt and Slater learned that there was good grass downstream from the spring, but they also read that ". . . there is something on which horses feed that poisons them" (p. 31) — undoubtedly the leeks. Thomas Turnbull wrote of this place: "their [sic] are a great many Springs all round here for about 20 Rod one at the bottom of the hill the best & coldest I ever drank off [sic] these springs make a pretty creek a little below . . ." (*Travels*, p. 218). Leek Spring is located near Leek Spring Lookout. Highway 88 bypasses it to the south and thus departs from the emigrant road, which ran north to Camp Creek. Wayman read in Platt and Slater: "From this spring you cross a ridge [Baltic Ridge] of some 2 miles in extent. The descent is very steep. You now have a somewhat better road, except some stony places. You descend a mountain more than a mile TO CAMP CREEK[.] . . . You do not cross Camp Creek, but turn from it to the right, up a long hill" (p. 31). That is to say, the road came to the head of the creek, which rises due north of Leek Spring. Thus avoiding the stream, which runs northwest, emigrants followed "up a long hill," which appears on topographical maps as Iron Mountain Ridge.

25

**Thursday AUG 26[th]** Well we started this morning, we did and made a drive of say 18 miles and are now nooning at Cold Springs[28] after passing over Otter Slide & pa[r]taking bountifully of Mellow beef stake after which we drove on over some d—d bad road and Ca[m]ped at the fork of the road, traveling 25 miles[.] Nothing to admire but the beautiful timber the tallest I ever saw[.] Pine and Fir and Arbor Vita[.]

---

[28] Cold Springs is on Iron Mountain Ridge. "No grass here," warned Platt and Slater (p. 31).

18

**Friday AUG 27[th]** We started this time from our last Cam[p]ing ground and made Hangtown[29] by 5 Oclock. Well this Hangtown is one of the towns what is a town[.] We sold out our interest in all Cattle and a glader boy never presented himself in this region[.] it is too late this evening to see much of the City so I will defer a further description until tomorrow[.]

---

[29] Placerville, California, located on U.S. 50 in El Dorado County. A description of the road leading here from Cold Springs appears in Platt and Slater, p. 32. When Mrs. Francis Sawyer arrived at Placerville, she wrote: "This is quite a lively place. There are numbers of miners here, and gold mines are near the town; some families have settled here, too" ("Overland to California," p. 18). The population in 1852, according to Henry S. Anable, was 4000 ("Journal," p. 73). The Sacramento *Union* of April 2, 1853, wrote of Placerville: "The site was

first settled in 1848 by William Daylor of Sutter's Fort and became known as Dry Diggings. In 1850 the camp was named Placerville because rich placers were discovered on near-by Weber Creek. The town never bore the name Hangtown, as is often asserted; this was simply a nickname given to it because of the speedy dispatch of three robbers on October 17, 1849" (Quoted in Eriven G. Gudde, *California Place Names*, p. 237). See also J. M. Letts, *California Illustrated*, p. 109. Dale Morgan gives the date of the lynching as sometime in January, 1849 (*Overland Diary of James A. Pritchard,* p. 171).

**Saturday AUG 28th** I woke up this morning and found somebody in the city of Hangtown went down stairs and look[ed] about took a snorte of Brandy and found out that it was "me" a matter that has been in dispute for some Months[.] I could not deside it satisfactorly: — for, I never drove cattle nor wa[l]ked bare footed through hot sand and dust; so the thing went on until this morning after washing myself & drinking about 3 inches — the matter was satisfacorly [sic] settled and I found that it was "me" *my self* forked and down right in the City of Hangtown California. Well I took an aspect of this place, and found it to be situated in a ravine long & crooked with but one street & that very norrow — some 2 or 3 M.s. containing some 3 or 4000 inhabitants made up of all kinds of people. They were mining all along the main ravine and several small ones pointing into the main one. Making tolerably good wages. Gambling going on by the whole sale.

**Sunday AUGUST 29th** This morning found "me" up and prepareing to leave for Sacramento city — the Hack Came in due time and I shiped aboard for $3.00 to S' city distance 50 miles. We drove 20 miles and bated at a good Tavern with as good grub as I wanted $100 [$1.00]. After we struck the American River 10 miles above the city I was delighted with the country[.] it is the most beautiful farming region that I ever saw any where. It looked like an old settled country, 1000 & 1000s as far as you could see was cultivated with some splinded residences[.] This appearance of the Valley of the American River continues down to the Main Sacramento Valley[.] Every thing here looks like living — — — Well about sundown we arrived in Sacramento[30] dusted off and eat a good supper and strolled about to see the city, heard the Church bells ring & saw good Christians going to sit under the dropings of the Sanctuary[.] went on a little further & found gambling Saloons plenty in full opperation, and all Kinds of evening business going on to suit customers &c, &c, &c.

[30] Sacramento grew up around Sutter's Fort after the discovery of gold in 1848 on the American River.

**Monday AUG 30th** This day was spent in looking around the city of Sacramento, Well it is a fine business place with a population of 13000[.]

88

AUGUST 1 - AUGUST 31, 1852

All kinds of work and trade are going on briskly. Some fine buildings now being finished. I have just finished a ramble to the Stage office to engage my passage to Stockton tomorrow[.] I am much pleased with the appearance of said city, though must keep rolling on, yet some further[.] Old Booth[31] plays to night in the Theatre R the 3rd — I have the best Health in the world[.]

[31] Wayman's reference to Booth as "Old Booth" suggests that he may have confused Edwin Booth (1822–93) with his famous father, Junius Brutus Booth (1796–1852). Edwin Booth performed in California in 1852 and, like his father, acted the role of Shakespeare's Richard III.

**Tuesday AUG 31st** To [*i.e.*, I] was occupied in traveling from here to Stockton[32] over as fine looking country as I ever saw in my life[.] The whole distance say 50 miles[.] Well in due time we were safely landed in Stockton City said to number 6000 souls and all kinds of Gambling as well as Work going on briskly[.] I am well pleased with this place — it is a good shipping place[33] and is improving fast with perminant buildings[.] Weather here is oppressively hot. all right I expect[.]

[32] Almost due south of Sacramento, Stockton is the seat of San Joaquin County. It is named for Commodore Robert Stockton (1795–1860), one-time self-appointed governor of California after he claimed it for the United States.

[33] The San Joaquin River connects Stockton with San Francisco Bay.

# September 1 – September 30, 1852

**Wednesday SEP 1st**  This day we made a start for Sonora and after traveling some 70 miles found our selves safely landed in said City[.][1] During our trip we passed over fine roads until we approached the Stanislaus River[2] where we nooned and changed Coaches for a tolerably rough road on to Sonora[.] Well we are here for the present & will do some prospecting soon of some kind. This City strongly reminds of Hangtown goodness[?][.]

---

[1] Sonora, California, the seat of Tuolumne County, is due east of Stockton. Mexicans from Sonora, Mexico, found rich gold deposits here in 1848. Located at the center of the Southern mining area, Sonora eventually saw more than six million dollars in gold taken from the mines in Tuolumne County. One of its citizens boasted the year before Wayman came that the camp had ". . . more gamblers, more drunkards, more ugly, bad women, and larger lumps of gold, and more of them, than any other place of similar dimensions within Uncle Sam's dominions" (Quoted in Remi Nadeau, *Ghost Towns and Mining Camps of California*, p. 100). A fire swept the town in June before Wayman's arrival.

[2] The Stanislaus River flows southeast out of the Sierra Nevada and joins the San Joaquin River south of Stockton. Sonora lies about five miles east.

**Thursday SEPT 2nd**  To day I spent looking around the town[.] Some mining going on but not extensively for the want of Water.— The whole face of the Country seems to be taken up in Claims[.] The town its self does not quite fill the bill as I expected[.] I am not yet satisfied and must look about a little more[.] No mail matter for me[;] this seems strange, but all right I expect[.]

I think that I will go to the river and see what is going on there soon as I can make it convenient to do so [.] Here I am [.]

**Friday SEPT[3] 3rd**  To day nothing else to do and nothing else to write about. I cleaned out my trunk & repacked my goods & chattles looking over my list of specimens[.] this is an awful hot day, yes oppressively so[.] I must arrange my notes & write home[.][4] I am becoming tired of doing nothing will soon

## SEPTEMBER 1 - SEPTEMBER 30, 1852

find some way to exersize myself[.] I think that I will go to Columbia[5] tomorrow and see how the land lies in that region[.] I am well as they make them in this region[.]

---

[3] *Sept* is written over *Aug*.

[4] No letter from this period has survived.

[5] Columbia is five miles directly north of Sonora. Eight stages connected the two towns (Nadeau, p. 95). Gold was discovered here in March, 1850, when the site was known as Hildreth's Diggings. "The honor of bestowing upon the camp its present name, Columbia, is due to Majors Farnsworth and Sullivan and Mr. D. G. Alexander, who formally named the place on the 29th of April" (Quoted in Eriven G. Gudde, *California Place Names*, p. 68). When Wayman was in Columbia in 1852, it was a thriving, rough-and-tumble community. There were banks, express offices, hotels, general stores (seventeen of them), fire companies, more than three dozen saloons, dance halls, and gambling joints — the whole lot representing a capital of nearly $2 million. There were also churches, book stores, a temperance organization (probably badly needed), a singing society, and theaters. See Nadeau, pp. 94–99.

**Saturday SEPT 4th** This very warm day has gone the way of all days and I am here feeling a little tired from the delay of working[.] I dislike to be lounging around in this style[.] Were it not for Miss Flavilla & Laura whose presence does beguile my time a little I don't know what would be the trumped — they are quite good looking girls and from Cincinnati — they seeme to be white folks. I have some disposition to go to Chruch to day   I don't know,

**Sunday SEPT 5th** I thought some of going to Church to [day] but after dressing myself and talking with Miss Flavilla awhile, I forgot Church matters until it was too late, so times are at present. I am now looking every day for my Miss Sophia to arrive from Stockton[.] she is a fine French girl, with very strong feelings and[6] Hell to talk. This evening I spent in prominading the streets & taking an *ASSpect* of the fashions   Mexican and Spanish women by the score, but very fiew American women, though go[o]d[?]. My fun I have had here[.]

---

[6] Inserted above the line is *I love her*.

**Monday SEPT 6th** Well I and M. T. started for the Stanislaus river to see what we could see. We proceted [*sic*] by the way of Shaw's Flat[7] where we unexpectedly found J. Lank[,] G. Whitman and A. J. Smith[.][8] leaving there, we proceeded far as Columbia and returned to Sonora again for Supper; postponing our trip to the river until a more convenient season. This days prospecting fills the bill very well. The appearance of the country and business prospects please me very well —

91

[7] A rich mining location in Tuolumne County midway between Sonora and Columbia. The site was originally an orchard owned by Mandeville Shaw (Gudde, p. 291).

[8] Lank's name reappears below in the entry for September 10. His full name was John A. Lank, and he lived at Shaw's Flat for many years. A. J. Smith may have been a partner of Lank in "the establishment of Smith, Lank & Co.," as indicated on a mortgage to the Mississippi House, September 20, 1852 (Letter to the editor from Mrs. George Eastman, November 8, 1968). G. Whitman remains unidentified. Possibly the initials *M.T.* at the beginning of this entry stand for McTrade.

**Tuesday SEPT 7th**  A cool night and a pleasant breezy day[.] Bill Loring came in last evening and is prominading about town with us to day[.] I am now wating the arrival of the Atlantic news before I write any more word to the East. Nothing going on here of special interest, and to make a change of kind I will make it in location or nothing else — this has been a very pleasant and bracing day, the most so of any since I have been in this region[.]

**Wednesday SEPT 8th**  I visited to Shaw's Flat and Springfield,[9] and returned again to Sonora to visit the Post office, before writing to the Atlantic States — as the Eastern News was due us here this day[.] Well I did, but found "nicht"[10] in wating for my portion[.] I am now going to scratch a line or two for the East and Wend my way to the Stanislaus river, and learn what is going on in that part of God's Moral Heritage[.]   this will do[.]

[9] Springfield was located about midway between Shaw's Flat and Columbia.

[10] *Nothing* in German.

**Thursday SEP 9th**  This day was spent writing to Hunt & Sim[11] and in loafing around town (Sonora). The weather here is perceptably warmer than it is in Indiana, and the dustiest country that I ever saw without exception, during the dry season. Tomorrow I want to go to the River (Stanislaus) and see what kind of an arrangement can be made there[.] I must soon Commence opperating Some where[.]
   3 or 4000 souls

[11] Wayman, writing to his brother Dr. James V. Wayman on April 23, 1852, from Indian Territory just west of St. Joseph, Missouri, mentions having written to them. These letters apparently have not survived. On the basis of a statement in a letter to his brother, June 12, 1854, it would appear that Sim was a partner of James Wayman in his medical practice in Cambridge City, Indiana. These letters are reproduced at the end of this volume. Hunt's name was James Hunt; see letter of August 2, 1858, note 5.

**Friday SEPT 10th**  Well, to day I and M. T. went over to Shaw's Flat and thence to Springfield, Columbia and Pass Lapine,[12] Stanislaus, saw nothing of much interest and returned to S's Flat and tabernacled for the night with

Mr Lank.— Making a very good day's travel considering the mountains and heat of the day. yet I discharged the task with Comparative ease, being used to journying[.]

---

[12] This is Wayman's rendition of Paso Del Pino, which was more commonly known as Pine Crossing and Pine Log Crossing. It was on the South Fork of the Stanislaus River north of Columbia in a deep gorge and was reached by a steep trail (Letter to the editor from Mrs. George Eastman, November 8, 1968).

**Saturday SEPT 11th** Through the solicitations of McFee[13] & G Whitman I visited Jamestown[14] some five miles south of Shaw's Flat, where I saw the Literati of Tuolomne County in Convention assembled preparatory to the nomination of suitable Candidates for the Senate and County officers — I saw no Websters nor H Clays among the crowd. Consequently I can't say anything of their fitness (*returned to Sonora*)[.]

---

[13] Unidentified.

[14] Jamestown was located in 1848 on Woods Creek southwest of Sonora by a San Francisco lawyer named Colonel George F. James. "After a series of disputes with Mexican settlers, which ended in James' ruin and departure, the name of the town was changed to American Camp, but later the old name was restored. Locally the place is known as 'Jimtown'" (Gudde, p. 147).

**Sunday SEPT 12th** This morning I got up I did — and forked around Sonora till breakfast was ready; I ate bountifully and picked myself up and found my way to Shaw's Flat where I remained during the day, taking an *asspicked* of the different trumps as turned, Nothing unusual occurred, but every thing seemed to occur in its usual place, such as Whiskey, Brandy, Gin & Wine — The News, a Confab and then a walk. O.K.

**Monday SEP 13[th]** This forenoon was spent in tramping around amonge the mines, but not to much purpose, Visiting Columbia during our pereg[r]inations[.] Returned and nooned at the F[l]at. And after settling our grub we concluded to visit Sonora, did so — and returned by supper time to the Flat again[.] Nothing occuring during the whole day worthey of special note. Considerable feeling manifested in relation to A Miners meeting to come off Saturday next.

**Tuesday SEPT 14th** I was very lazy this good day, and in consequence did but little or rather nothing in the way of prospecting or any thing else, other than indulging a species of Dogged laziness — The air to day is some cooler than it has been for several days past, and yet it seems quite too warm for confort [*sic*]. I am slowly learning the fashions of California which every one must do before he can operate to much advantage independent of fool luck[.]

**Wednesday SEPT 15th**  I rose, washed and dressed myself this morning, and breakfasted — picked up an [*sic*] newspaper, lay my carcass down and read the news, Feeling som[e]what indisposed I Kept in doors all day. The sky this evening looks hazy and the Horizen dim and smoky, in many respects like Indian summer in the Eastern States. The sun is now sinking behind the Western M.s. lending a dull, red color to the W— Horizen, while the miners are wending their way from their work in different directions[.]

**Thursday SEPT 16th**  Remained in the city all day to day, feeling some little indisposed and awful lazy and indolent. The weather is warm and dry yet with cool nights. This Kind of weather seems to me would be favorable to the production of Bilious diseases; it would in the Atlantic States I am Certain. People here seem to be more disposed to laziness than I expected.— Indeed I feel considerable so inclined my self. this is quite Common[.]

**Friday SEPT 17[th]**  This morning, I found my way down to Sonora and shiped my Trunk, Blanket, rugg and Traps for Shaw's Flat; took a fiew turns up and down the street, taking a general Asspect of the city, improvements, and fashinos [*sic*]— took a snort and left. Times [*sic*] drags slowly by having but little to care for or regret. I hope to soon have an opportunity to relieve his way of going over time's road[.]

**Saturday SEPT 18[th]**  Went to Jamestown this morning to the Convention Called by the Miners of Tuolomne county —[15] Felt somewhat indesposed, head aches &c — and Concluded to return home, did so and spent the balance of the day lounging about to no purpose[.] took a portion of Med — I am quite tired of this dullness — and expect and hope soon to have an opportunity to make a happy change[.]

---

[15] The meeting to which Wayman refers was aimed at preventing foreign labor, especially Chinese, from invading the southern mines. Similar meetings were held in other mining communities (Letter from Mrs. George Eastman to the editor, October 23, 1968). Wayman refers to the Jamestown meeting above; see diary entry for September 13. He seems to have sided with the native miners, as indicated by his remarks against "the d—d Foreign portion" in his diary entry for September 21.

**Sunday 19th**  This day was passed lazily away, as Sunday is usually spent. No church to visit, and consequently have to be my own interpreter — though, I am satisfied with my condition so far as that matter is Concerned[.] The weather is some cooler and agreeable — more[.] The atmosphere looks dull and hazy and Smoky; betokening as I think rain soon — times are going on on on and still on[.]

**Monday SEPT 20[th]**   A pleasant day this, visited Sonora and returned home again. I am slowly becoming acquainted with California and California people — The fashions are a strong shade different from the eastern States — though the difference is not in favor of this region. Some very fine men here — While the great majority are of the worst possible cast. Indeed it seems unnatural that so fine a country should[.]

**Tuesday SEPT 21[st]**   Weather fine and pleasant — Sky, yet dull smoky and threatning. This is one of the finest countries in the World settled or inhabited with a mongrel race of beings, made up from all quarters of the Globe, and well calculated to ruin and morally damn any country. Society here in most places is awfully depraved, and will forever remain so, so long as the d—d Foreign portion is allowed to remain[.]

**Wednesday SEPT 22[nd]**   Quite cool last night and during this day. I took, this morning a ramble with Dr Butler[16] among the Mountains, but found nothing worthey either of notice or preservation. Since which I have spent the day walking and looking around among the fashions of the Flat[.] The weather seems to have taken a permanent change, being quite cool with a fair prospect of remaining so. A smoky hazy atmosphere,— Indian summer in full.

---

[16] Unidentified.

**Thursday SEPT 23rd**   Days are still fine and cool, while the nights are very cool, requiring double covering. I again, in company with Mr Cooper[17] and Dr Butler, tramped among the mountains till noon to day; during which time, we passed several mining locations some of which, looked very favorable according to my judgement of such things. I am yet unimployed as to actual work, Yet I think that I will soon be situated among the Dirt, water, mud and I hope Gold —

---

[17] On the basis of information from Mrs. George Eastman, this may have been William H. Cooper, who was well known in Sonora. In 1850 he and another man named Gulledge surveyed the town and laid out lots. In 1852 he was in the livery business in Sonora (Letter from Mrs. Eastman to the editor, November 13, 1968).

**Friday SEPT 24[th]**   This forenoon, went down to Sonora, and found no mail matter, returned and eat my Grub. The afternoon was passed off to no purpose as usual, not being anything offered to alter the program. Yet the prospect is pretty good for a faverable change — The weather is quite cool and bracing and I would suppose very healthy. Yet I have to take a little med[icine] to Keep right[.]

**Saturday SEPT 25th** Hearing that the mail had arrived bringing News from the States, I again visited Sonora, expecting to hear from Cambridge city, but was again disapointed, not receiving any thing in the shape of letter, paper, or Telegraph news —[18] W[h]ile I am in no Hell of a hobble about it, and Consequently will go on my way rejoicing as usual, I s[t]ill have a few trumps left and am ready and willing to play them, when opportunity offers[.]

[18] A constant complaint in Wayman's surviving letters is the failure of his relatives in Indiana to write to him.

**Sunday SEPT 26[th]** I spent this day, in writing to G. W. Boman and E. Vinton,[19] What time was not thus spent, was spent in Company with McPherson[20] in his sick room[.] From where I was located at my writing desk I could hear the sonous [sonorous] sound of the minister's voice warning sinners of the eror [sic] of their ways[;] good man, and in a good Cause for which he will be richly rewarded some time maybe, A fine clear day, all right[.]

[19] Boman remains unidentified, although he may have been a friend in Indiana. Vinton is Eldridge Vinton, with whom Wayman had left Cambridge City on March 25.
[20] Probably this is Wayman's cross-country companion referred to in earlier parts of the diary as "Mc." His name appears in Wayman's expense account under the dates of August 5 and 12; see pp. 104–105.

**Monday SEPT 27[th]** Well times run by as usual — Nothing of interest on hands [sic]. Still waiting the moution[21] of the Miners Committe[e][.] I am in a d—d disagreeable mood in Consequence of this cursed delay, but cant help it, time must & will work out its own course — and then I will make an effort to work out my interest in this good region of God's moral heritage at least I will make an effort to do so &c &c.

[21] Wayman may have intended to write *motion*, although the actual letters are either as they appear above or *montive*.

**Tuesday SEPT 28[th]** Here I am and here we go as usual, not any thing done yet or likely to be soon. So things generally work when one has to depend upon the movements of others[.] M Trade[22] is quiled [?] up with an attack of Varioloid,[23] and will be unfit to attend to business for some days. After which I presume that some thing else will be the trump — I Cant say, but will wait the issue &c —

[22] Although Wayman has written *M Trade* here, his diary entry for October 4 gives the name as McTrade. This individual remains unidentified, but he must have been a mutual acquaintance of both Wayman and his brother James V. Wayman; see letter of April 23, 1852, in which Wayman says he met "M. Trade" in St. Louis.
[23] A mild form of smallpox.

## SEPTEMBER 1 - SEPTEMBER 30, 1852

**Wednesday SEPT 29[th]**  I am forking around, and looking about, to see all I can see, for it Seems as though I am destined not [to] have an opportunity to work for some time to Come, how soon I Cant say and am growing quite indiffere[n]t — I am reading in the mean time and making some acquaintances which will be all right in good time if I remain in this region[.]

**Thursday SEPT 30[th]**  I have visited quite a number of mining locations, to see how times are working in this important calling, as I hope soon to be a member of that honorable portion of [the] Community[.] It is quite pleasant to ramble about here and observe the different formations, and features of the Mountains[.] I Could spend my time very agreeably if necessity did not intrude[.]

# October 1, 1852 – March 25, 1853

**Friday OCT 1[st]** My time is passing rapidly by and not any thing yet done Only in the way of observation which I don't think lost by any means — yet I should feel much better pleased if I were situated in some rich hole working as I ought to be, and hope soon to realize. I wish that I was a good and true prophit, so that I might take a peep on the other side a moment[.]

**Saturday OCT 2[nd]** Morning Came and found me up waiting my breakfast, as usual. I am in possession of one of the d—dst appetites in this region and feel quite well[;] this is all that I have to brag of and feel tolerably thankful that I have no more room to grumble[.] I could render thanks for a d—d site more in the Same time[.]

**Sunday OCT 3rd** The Lord's day once more. I would go to church to day, if I had any encouragement that I would be paid for my trouble. Every thing is done here for wages, and I find that I must learn the fashion to keep in company with the ballance. Not having the assurance Spoken of I chose to Stay at home and read my book like a good boy[.] Fine day, cool and pleasant as could be wished — —

**Monday OCT 4[th]** This morning I, McTrade & Company concluded to take a prospecting tour, and locate our selves for the Season. We did so, but found no encouragement and returned. During our tramp Col Whitman[1] Killed a fine buck, which was quite a treat in its line. Returning we crossed the table mountain, which I found to be covered with Amygdaloid Augite Rock.

---

[1] Probably G. Whitman, whom Wayman mentions in his diary entry for September 6.

**Tuesday OCT 5[th]** Well this good day was whiled away in reading, walking and talking — The Weather is and has been for some 6 days past cloudy and

## OCTOBER 1, 1852 - MARCH 25, 1853

threatning. From the present indications I presume that rain will Come soon, the Small streams are swelling — a certain sign of rain some where. It is very, very dry here now[.]

**Wednesday OCT 6[th]**   Today is more pleasant[.]

**Thursday OCT 7[th]**   Nothing done of consequence

**Friday OCT 8[th]**   As usual hard up

**Saturday OCT 9[th]**   Same story yet

**Sunday OCT 10[th]**   passed reading &c

**Monday OCT 11[th]**   Bothered as usual with d—d-Mexicans

**Tuesday OCT 12[th]**   Day s[p]ent in visiting the sick &c &c — —

**October 13th**

**Wednesday 13th**   Worked a little

**Thursday 14[th]**   Mined it all day

**Friday 15[th]**   The same —

**Saturday 16[th]**   Worked some[.]

**Sunday 17[th]**   Fine warm day

**Mond[a]y 18[th]**   Good weather for work

**Tuesday 19[th]**   yet dry

**Wednesday OCT 20[th]**   no rain yet

**Thursday 21[st]**   rain wanted by the miners

**Friday 22[nd]**

**Saturday 23[rd]**

**Sunday 24[th]**

Monday 25[th]

Tuesday 26[th]

Wednesday 27[th]

Thursday 28[th]

Friday 29[th]

Saturday 30[th]

Sunday 31[st]   Fine day all right

Monday NOV 1[st]

Tuesday " 2[nd]

Wednesday 3[rd]

Thursday 4[th]

Friday 5[th]

Saturday 6[th]   The atmosphere looks dull and threatning[.]

Sunday 7[th]   Signes [sic] of rain

Monday 8[th]   windy and some Clouds floating

Tuesday 9[th]   Cloudy

Wednesday 10[th]   Worked some to day[.] made litter [little?]

Thursday 11[th]   worked upon the claim today —

Friday 12[th]   Today visit[ed] by a deligation from Sonora, dispossessed us.

Saturday 13[th]   this morning M- whaled a dutchman like Hell[.]

Sunday 14[th]   The rain is coming to town quite freely[.] rain

Monday 15[th]   rain and wind

# OCTOBER 1, 1852 - MARCH 25, 1853

**Tuesday 16[th]**   wind and rain

**Wednesday 17[th]**   Strong wind from the south & rain

**Thursday 18[th]**   Showers with strong wind

**Friday 19[th]**   rain and mud plenty

**Saturday 20[th]**   Threatning clouds and some rain all day

**Sunday 21[st]**   During the afternoon & night rain in abundance

**Monday 22[nd]**   It rained faithfully all day and night — the Earth is saturated with water[.]

**Tuesday 23[rd]**   Cloudy, gloomy and drizzly all day

**Wednesday 24[th]**   No rain to day, for the first [time] during a week or more.

**Thursday 25[th]**   Frosty mornings, and fair days — fine weather this — though very muddy.

**Friday NOV 26[th]**   A very fine clear day, I went to Sonora for med[icine] & letters, but found neither. *soupe* for dinner. White frost this morning.

**Saturday 27[th]**   Warm & cloudy, every indication of rain. The wind from the south a sure index to rain

**Sunday 28[th]**   It Commenced raining last night, and has Continued to do so all day, with flattering prospects ahead for the same[.] In obedience to the fates that haunt my path I have not heard one word from home yet. I am very well & will make my way without[.]

**Monday, 29th 1852**   One continued ceaseless days rain, with a constant strong gale from the south. It is now as muddy as could be wished, with flattering prospects for an increased supply. This is all in the bill.

**Tuesday, NOV 30th**   The rain of yesterday increased as night came on, and one ceaseless torent raged the whole night long. This morning seems disposed to continue the attack[.] rained all day.

**Wednesday DEC 1st 1852**   Rain at regular intervals all day — Nothing unusual on hand. The Heavens dark and threatning, times gloomy.—

**Thursday 2nd**  Cloudy and gloomy all day, southwest wind

**Friday 3rd**  No rain to day, but every indication for a protracted one, scored timber to day for house[.]

**Saturday 4th**  Rain all day long  Muddy, Muddy —

**Sunday 5th**  Today it rained until noon. The afternoon was quiet, with some indications of clear weather[.]

**Monday 6th**  A very fine sunny day. A fiew Clouds floating high. Quite warm and pleasant

**Tuesday 7th**  Pleasant and sunny during the forenoon  cloudy and threatning the afternoon and night

**Wednesday 8th 1852**  A fine day, some cloudy though warm & pleasant

**Thursday 9th**  Some cloudy to day though warm and fine[.] Our claim changed hand[s] again to day, but changed back immediately[.]

**Friday 10[th]**  Some cloudy though pleasant

**Saturday 11[th]**  drunk to day  fine day  mirkey and dull at evening

**Sunday 12[th]**  Alternating, sun and cloud threatning

**Monday 13[th]**  today[2]

---

[2] Before *today* the word *regular* and one illegible word are crossed out.

**Tuesday 14[th]**  Snow all day & night

OCTOBER 1, 1852 - MARCH 25, 1853

**Wednesday 15th**   snow all day[3]   cloudy   windy

[3] The words *snow all day* are written over several words that Wayman crossed out.

| | |
|---|---|
| Citric Acid ½ lb | 1.00 |
| Diary 2 [at] 40 cts | 80 |
| Med Pocketbook | 2.00 |
| One ax[4] | 1.25 |
| Whiskey & ferriage at Fort Laramie | 75 |
| Camp Kettle | 2.50+ |
| To Loring at Ash-hollow | 1.00 |
| Coffee Pot | 1.25 |
| Hams | 4.00 |
| Ferriage | 25 |
| Salt on the Platte | 1.00 |
| Buffaloe Robe | 1.50 |
| Lanitte Lariat | 50 |
| Flour 50 lbs | + 5.00 |
| Ferriage over Sweet Water | 1 00 |
| Black Lead | + 75 |
| Ferriage over Green River | 4.25 |
| Toll over Thomas' Fork | 1.00 |
| For Whiskey at toll bridge | 75 |
| Moccasins | 1 00 |
| | 31 55 |
| For Buffaloe Robe | $5.00 |
| For Horse Shoe nails | 50 |
| For Whiskey | 1.00 |
| For Whiskey at Green River | 50 |
| For oxen near Oregon [town] Mo | 70 00 |
| Expences during trip | 5 00 |
| One pair Moccasins | 50 |
| July 7th  1 bushel potatoes | 3 00 |
| "  9  Corn Meal | 2 00 |
| "  10  McPherson cash | 1.00 |
| "  29  For Meat | 2.00 |
| "  "  Mc—to cash— | 50 |
| Aug 3rd  For Whiskey (sink) | 3.00 |
| "  4  Do— Desert | 1.50 |
| "  5  For Meat | + 4.00 |
| "  "  Whiskey Raggtown | 50 |
| "  "  McPherson | 1 00 |
| "  6  Whiskey Beef Market | 50 |
| "  7  Do— | 50 |
| "  Whiskey at Ash Hollow | 1.50 |
| "  9 & 10[?] Whiskey & pies | 2.00 |
| | 105.50 |

# OCTOBER 1, 1852 - MARCH 25, 1853

[Recto of back flyback]
Carson Valley
August 12th

|   |   |   |
|---|---|---|
|  | Whiskey | 25 |
|  | MacPherson to | $8.00 |
| 13 | To cash | 2.50 |
| Aug " | cash paid for flour | 12.00+ |
| 16 | For Whiskey self | 75 |
|  | For bread in camp | 50 |
| 17 | Whiskey self – – | 50 |
| 19 | "            " | 1.00 |
| 20 | "            " | 1.00 |
| 21 | ------------------------ | 75 |
| 22 | ------------------------ | 50 |
| 23 | ------------------------ | 50 |
| " | Toll over bridges | 1.00 |
| 24 | meat | + 75 |
| 25 | Flour | + 2.50 |
|  | Whiskey | 1.50 |
| 26 | Meat | + 1.60 |
| 27 | Hay | + 2.20 |
|  | Whiskey | 1.50 |
| 28 | Shirts & Shave | 10.50 |
|  |  | 49.80 |

[Verso of back flyleaf]

```
     49.80
    105.50
     31.55
    ------
    $186.85
```

---

[4] Between this and the next line, Wayman wrote *East – 2 Boxes*[?] followed by 50 in the column of figures at the right and then crossed out the entire line.

**Thursday – 16th**  8 inches of snow this morning, *and raining*

**Friday 17[th]**  rain all day and all night –

**Saturday 18[th]**  Still raining with flattering prospects for a sett[l]ed rain –––

**Sunday 19th**  Some rain during the fore noon. Cloudy and sunshine alternated this evening [?]

105

[Inside of back cover]

|  |  |  |  |
|---|---|---|---|
| 25 |  |  | 31.55 |
| 27 |  |  | 88.50 |
| 15 |  |  | 120.05 |
| 24 |  |  | 200 |
| 25 |  |  | 24 |
| 25 | 1888 |  | 344.05 |
| 23 | 1889 |  | 75 |
| 24 |  |  | 1.25 |
| 19 | 339 |  | 75 |
| 22 | 274 |  | 1.00 |
| 24 | 65 |  | 50 |
| 21 |  |  | 3.00 |
| 274 |  |  | 1.50 |
|  |  | 25 | 50 |
| 12.00 |  | 27 | 50 |
| 101.50 |  | 18 | 50 |
| 31.55 |  | 24 | 10.25 |
| 155.05[5] |  | 25 |  |
| 224 |  | 25 |  |
| 379.05 [error for 369.05] | | 23 | |
|  |  | 24 |  |
|  |  | 19 |  |
|  |  | 22 |  |
|  |  | 24 |  |
|  |  | 24 |  |
|  |  | 280 |  |
|  |  | 28 |  |
|  |  | 308 |  |

[5] An error for 145.05.

[Inside front cover]

**Monday DECR 20th [1852]**   A beautifully sunny day – – –

**Tuesday 21st**   Snowed till noon, and same the afternoon

# OCTOBER 1, 1852 - MARCH 25, 1853

**Wednesday 22nd**   6 inches of snow this morning, snowing all day, and *thawing*[.] [for?][6] the first letters[.]

---

[6] One word illegible. Possibly Wayman intended *Rec'd*.

**Thursday 23rd**   Snowed till noon after rain the ballance [of the] day[.]

**Friday 24th 1852**   Snow and rain all day

[Recto of front flyleaf]

**Saturday 25th**   snowed all last night & to day awful.

**Sunday 26[th]**   snow and rain all day —

**Monday 27[th]**   Clear and fine

**Tuesday 28th 1852**   rain all day long

**Wednesday 29th**   one continued shower all day —

**Thursday 30[th]**   High clouds and some fine rain   little broken

**Friday 31st**   One continued rain all day.

**Saturday JAN 1st 1853**   This morning the clouds run [ran?] high, some indications of cl[e]aring up

**Saturday 22nd JAN**[7]   Clear fine warm day

---

[7] Wayman wrote the following diary entries on two folded sheets of paper which he placed in the pocket of the diary. They appear to have been written while he was still in Tuolumne County. The entries between January 1 and 22 are missing.

**Sunday 23rd JAN**   Warm and some cloudy though fine

**Monday 24[th] JAN**   Hazy though warm and fine

**Tuesday 25th**   Warm & clear cool nights

**Wednesday 26[th]**   Some Cloudy and warm.

**Thursday 27th**   Still warm and cloudy looks much like rain —

Friday 28[th]   moderate rain all day

Saturday 29th   Sunny and warm

Sunday — Warm and — 30th [sic] pleasant   some cloudy

Monday 31st 1853   Some rain during the morning — Cloudy and warm into evening

Tuesday FEB 1st, 1853   Warm and clear — 60°

Wednesday Feb 2nd   Quite fine   glorious &c
Very clear and pleasant
Still and warm 60°

Frosty nights

Thursday FEB 3rd   Clear & warm ——— 60°

Friday FEB 4[th] — Clear   warm   60° again

Saturday FEB 5[th]   Good clear day — Glorious weather 60°

Frosty nights

Sunday FEB 6th   Clear day   warm

Monday FEB 7th   fine warm & pleasant 62°

Tuesday 8[th]   63°   fair all day

Wednesday 9[th]   Fair & fine   67° —

Thursday 10[th]   Still fair

Friday 11th   fine

Saturday 12th   fair day   pleasant

Sunday warm   13th

Monday 14th 1853   warm & clear   65

Tuesday 15[th]   clear

Wednesday 16[th]   warm   65°

## OCTOBER 1, 1852 - MARCH 25, 1853

**Thursday 17[th]**   clear

**Friday 18[th]**   clear   65

**Saturday 19[th]**   fine

**Sunday 20[th]**   fine

**Monday 21[st]**   some cloudy

**Tuesday 22[nd]**   fine

**Wednesday 23[rd]**   fine

**Thursday 24[th]**   Cloudy

**Friday 25[th] 1853**   rained some – – –

**Saturday 26[th]**   cloudy some   rain in night

**Sunday 27[th]**   fine & warm

**Monday 28[th] & last**   Clear and warm

**MARCH 1st 1853**   Tuesday fine and Clear — little murky

**Wednesday 2nd**   fine

**Thursday 3rd**   warm[8]

---

[8] Wayman struck out two entries which followed here. The first reads: "Wednesday 4 Ball at Columbia[.]" The second reads: "Thursday March 5   good day[.]"

**Friday 4th**[9]

---

[9] Wayman's correction for *5th*, which he crossed off.

**Saturday 5th**[10]

---

[10] A correction for *6*, which he crossed off.

**Sunday 6th**[11]

---

[11] A correction for *7*, which he crossed off.

109

## A DOCTOR ON THE CALIFORNIA TRAIL

**Monday 7th**[12]

[12] A correction for 8, which he crossed off.

**Tuesday 8[th]** — rain

**Wednesday — 9[th]** — rain

**Thursday 10th** fair & cool

**Friday 11[th]** cool some cloudy

**Saturday 12[th]** clear

**Sunday 13[th]** clear & frosty

**Monday MARCH 14[th]**

**Tuesday 15[th]**

**Wednesday 16[th]**

**Thursday 17[th]**

**Friday 18[th]** fine

**Saturday 19[th]**

**Sunday 20[th]**

**Monday 21[st]**

**Tuesday 22[nd]** —

**Wednesday 23rd**

**Thursday 24[th]**

**Friday 25[th]**

# Letters
## OF DR. JOHN H. WAYMAN TO DR. JAMES V. WAYMAN

The six letters which appear in the following pages were enclosed in the pocket of Wayman's diary at the time Mr. Rosenstock purchased it from Mrs. Wayman E. Ballenger. They cover a period of six years, from the spring of 1852, when Wayman was encamped temporarily on the west side of the Missouri River a week before starting across the plains, until he had taken up residence as a physician in Carson City, Nevada, early in 1862.

A few additional letters not included here are in the possession of Mrs. Ballenger. Only two of these have I seen. The earliest was written from Forest City, California, on January 26, 1857, in reply to a letter from his brother James written on December 4, 1856. Like the letter of August 2, 1858, printed here, it shows that his brother had been the victim of public gossip and slander, but the circumstances of these accusations are not clearly evident. The letter also shows that Wayman was, as he put it, "making money," although not from his mining investments. In addition, his brother had apparently suggested that he go with him to Cuba in the spring; Wayman rejected this proposal. The reason for the Cuban visit is not clear, but it may have had something to do with the demands of expansionists that the United States seize Cuba from Spain. Writing that the country had never "achieved a greater victory," Wayman also comments approvingly upon the election of James Buchanan as President in the previous November campaign. The rest of the letter (it is incomplete) gives evidence of Wayman's strong anti-Negro feeling and expresses his annoyance concerning the interest which his brother Milton, a clergyman, showed for Negroes as well as his association with the Republican party. The same attitude appears in his letter of August 2, 1858, which is printed here.

The second of the two letters is also directed to his brother James from Forest City, July 15, 1857. It shows that at this time he intended to visit his relatives in Cambridge City, Indiana, in the coming spring, but he writes that he could never again be content to live there. The letter also reflects his interest in Free Masonry and indicates that he was a member of the lodge in Forest City. But chiefly it is about the cities of San Francisco and Sacramento, both of which he had recently visited for the first time in two years. He predicted that San Francisco would become one of the most important cities in the United States and praised it for its broad, paved streets, new buildings, and lighting. But he reserved his highest praise for Sacramento, which he regarded as being superior to San Francisco in its refined society, thriftiness, beauty, taste, elegance, and public spirit. He intended to make one or the other his permanent home, he stated, if he decided to remain in California much longer.

The diary gives evidence that Wayman wrote additional letters from the southern mines after his arrival there late in 1852, and the diary entry for Sunday, June 6, 1852, shows that he wrote a letter to James from Fort Laramie, which Wayman and his party had reached the day before on their journey to California. This letter is also in Mrs. Ballenger's possession, but unfortunately I have been unable to see it. It most likely contains an interesting account of his trip up to this point in the journey.

The six letters given here, however, enable us to see details in Wayman's life not revealed in the diary, to which they are a valuable supplement.

※ ※ ※

Indian Territory, Tent N° 1 — April 25th [1852]

Bro J. V. Wayman,

I left Cincinnati the 31st of March, and arrived at St Louis the Sunday following: Nothing occured during the trip worthy of note, save the gentlemanly treatment of the Captain and officers — they are fine fellows, we lived well and had a pleasant time. I found M. Trade[1] at St Louis as expected *all right*. On Wednesday April the 7th, we shiped on board the steamer Clipper, No. 2 bound for St. Joseph. And were luckey enough to find a very good set of officers: The Captain and first Clerk were Odd-Fellows — Notwithstanding the tediousness of the trip, we spent out time pleasantly — We were Eleven days making the run from St Louis to St Joseph, a distance of 550 miles. Arrived at St Jo — Saturday the 17th[.]

Next day being sunday we packed our *Kit* and went into Camp, and have been enjoying Camp life since. Friday the 23 we crossed the river[2] and took a location in the Indian Territory where we will remain until we leave for the Plains. I think that we will make a move the first week in May, if so I am satisfied. — We are fiting up an Ox team for provisions and bagage and a light Cart and horse extra, for such purposes as sircumstances may demand. The emigration is not as great as I expected — Persons living here say that it is not half[3] what it was in 1850 — indeed I am agreeably disapointed in the number at this point —

---

[1] Wayman mentions him later during his stay at Shaw's Flat, California; see his diary entries for September 28 and October 4. In the latter entry he spells his name *McTrade*.

[2] The Missouri River.

[3] Two or three illegible words are crossed out after *half*.

I am told that the main rush is at Council Bluffs, about 180 miles above this place — One third of the emigrants so far as I can learn, is going to Oregon. Every 3rd tent in our vicinity, has women and children, some for California and others for Oregon[.]

The weather has been very cold and disagreeable for some weeks past — it is a very backward spring so far — Yesterday evening a fine shower of rain fell, and this morning is clear and fine, but yet too cool — We are all in fine health, and able for double rations, indeed I never felt better, with an appitite like a saw Mill. Maston Campbell[4] is our cook — We have good grub — Sleep well, live well, feel well, and expect to do *well* —

Coming down the river from Cincinnati, I became acquainted with an elderly gentleman who gave me a history of Uncle Sol Wayman's property — He says that Uncle Sol has sold three different lots off the farm, and the purchacers have recently learned that there is an old Mortgage not satisfied, and consequently refuse to make any further payments — it is creating quite an excitement amonge them[.] This old gentleman of whom I speak seemed to know all about it, and wanted to buy of me, my interest in the Mortgage. He was very inquisitive about the number of heirs, and the probable course they would take in the matter — He spoke of going out to see Mother & you about it — The County having been divided, and the old record not Examined those men who bought did not know till very lately that anything of the kind existed, and now refuse to make payment until this Mortgage is sati[s]fied[.] The ground was sold at the rate of 100$ per acre. You will send this word to Mother — I think that it would [be] well enough to see unto the matter and see how the land lies[.] For further particulars in relation to my perigrinations see Hunt[5] and Sim's letter[.] I will write you again from Fort Carney — Truly

J. H. Wayman

---

[4] He is not mentioned in the diary and is otherwise unidentified.

[5] His full name was James Hunt; but other than the fact that he was an acquaintance of Wayman, he remains unidentified; see below, letter to J. V. Wayman, August 2, 1858, where Wayman refers to him as Jim Hunt.

Forest City California
June 12th, 1854

Bro J. V. Wayman,

Your word of February last was recived some weeks ago, but not in time for the departure of the last Steamers, consequently I have deferd writing till the present, and even now I have not anything of importance to tell you, other than I am settled for the present, and will make no more moves until I move towards home. I suppose that you have long since received my word, written while I was at Panama,[1] giving you an outline of my perigrinations &c —. Well, since, I have changed my Programme, and now find myself in, and among the mountains again. I left Panama on the first of April, with the intention of finding my way to Guaymas Mexico. Not meeting with an apportunity of sailing direct to that port, I concluded to stop at Acapulco and take the chances to my destination[.] Well, on arriving at Acapulco I found every thing alive with fear, anxiety and excitement. Santa Ana[2] and forces were within a fiew leagues of the city, and every preparation was being made for the defence of the town. Strangers were looked upon with mistrust and suspicion, in short every thing conspired to make it anything but a desireable place to halt, consequently I chose to extend my voyage to San Francisco, I arrived in the Bay City on the evening of the 14th April, per Steamer Golden Gate, in good order and well conditioned. Here I made up my mind to spend the summer in the north, and in obedience to this resolution I shipped my cargo and Carcass for Marysville,[3] and thence to Forest City[4] (my present home) situated about 60 miles north of Marysville between[5] the north and middle Yubas. I saw A Hannah in San Francisco, on his way home, you no doubt have

---

[1] Wayman had returned to Cambridge City, Indiana, for a visit, but just when he left California for this purpose is not evident. To reach Panama he could have taken a ship from New York, but more likely he embarked from New Orleans after traveling down the Ohio and Mississippi rivers on a steamer.

[2] Antonio López de Santa Anna (1795?–1876), who in 1854 was dictator of Mexico.

[3] Marysville is located forty miles due north of Sacramento in Yuba County. During Wayman's time it was an important center of supplies for the surrounding mining areas.

[4] Forest City is located in Sierra County about four and a half miles southwest of Downieville, the county seat. Gold was discovered here in 1852 or '53 by Michael Savage. At this time the site was called Forks of Oregon Creek. Later it bore the names Yomana, Marietta, and Elizaville. The name *Forest City* is derived from the given name of Mrs. Forest Mooney, who settled here in 1854 with her husband, Captain Mooney. Articles which she contributed to Marysville newspapers bore the dateline "Forest City." The present name is Forest. See Phil P. Hanna, comp., *Dictionary of California Land Names*, pp. 108–109. See also *Knight's Scrapbook*, p. 73; *Hutchings' Illustrated California Magazine*, III, 104; *Illustrated History of Plumas, Lassen & Sierra Counties*, pp. 473–76; and *Quarterly of the Society of California Pioneers*, VI, 183.

[5] Following *between*, Wayman crossed off the words *the forks of*.

seen him ere this, I found J. T. Bloomfield, Charly McLaughlin and Charles Henry in Marysville. I was there but one night with them. McLaughlin is a *rich* man.

I have recently bought an interest in a mining claim, which I *think* will pay something very handsome — I Can make at the practice,[6] at least enough to keep myself and hire a hand to work. This is the condition that I have been seeking since my arrival in California. It now remains for time to tell the story — I am in the richest mining district in California and yet, it is here as elsewhere, many very many destitute — *strapped*. If you had never been here, I would undertake the picture —[7] here I will hold — In answer to your inquiry as to the time I will return home, I will say that I have made up my mind to visit Cambridge City next Spring, nothing occuring in the mean time to prevent — and you *know* that I am not apt to change, when I have once made up my mind. I think that a voluntary exile of 3 years is sufficient to satisfy any reasonable appitite, for the New, strange and marvelous — I am well pleased with my trip South, as indeed I am with my tour to California, and hope to profit by it through all coming life. A ramble of this character is not time lost to the close observer, aside from money matters[.] I have been roving about so long, and shifting my location so often, that I am quite satisfied, with this kind of life, hence the disposition I feel for home and rest. Yet this is all referable to stringent money matters, you ought to know how this is. Indeed if I were able, nothing in life would suit me better than a trip to some foreign Country — Enough of this — I am pleased to hear of the improvements going on in Cambridge & vicinity. It does not surprise me to learn that you have starved Sim[8] out, and have every thing in the practice[9] your own way, this is all natural, and just as I would suppose, if you wished it — I received a letter from Bro William at the same time that yours came to hand. I will write him by next mail — Tell Juliet[10] that I positively *will* write her by the next mail. I ought to have written her long since,[11] during my southern tour, I was not in[12] a writing mood — I want you to write me by return mail and give me the New Castle[13] news and all else that you please — You will send your letters to San Francisco[.] We have no Post office in this place, and I could get my mail matter from San Francisco [as] easy as any other point[.]

Yours Truly<br>J. H. Wayman

---

[6] His medical practice.

[7] This sentence refers to his brother's visit to California in 1849.

[8] This is the person referred to in the previous letter (April 12, 1852) and also in the diary entry of September 9, 1852.

[9] His brother's medical practice. Apparently Sim was a partner.

[10] Wayman's seventeen-year-old niece, the daughter of his brother James.

[11] Following *since*, Wayman wrote *but* and then crossed it off.

[12] Following *in*, he wrote *the* but then crossed it off.

[13] New Castle, Henry County, Indiana.

Forest City California
April 25th, 1855

Bro J. V. Wayman,

A few days ago I received two letters from your hand, the first that I have read from home, since my residence in Forest City. One bearing date Feb 13th the other March 4th 55. You spoke of other letters written by your self and our folks at New Castle. I have not received one word from any one of the tribe Since my debut in this place, save your self[.] Indeed, I thought it very strange that you didnot [sic] respond to my word; I had fully made up my mind never to write again to any of you. I am always willing, and even anxious to write you, but it annoys me very much to have my letters remain unanswered. I wrote Bro William soon after receiving his last word, which was in May 1854, Since which time I have not heard a syllable, save your word above named. I wrote you while I was at Panama — at San Francisco and Since my stay in this place. About this time, I wrote Juliet, and directed to College Hill. I wonder if she received it[.] It seems very strange indeed, that all of your letters should be miss laid. So much for Correspondence. Well, let it all go, with the hope that such Circumstances may never occur again. I did think of Coming home this Spring, but I have made up my mind to remain one year longer among the mountains and see what trump will turn up. I can't think of leaving my interests in California at the present time. It seems to me that I have just become sufficiently acquainted with *Cal.* life and the attending etceteras, to make it profitable to stay awhile longer. Were it not for my chances in the Mines, I would not stay in the mountains a week longer, indeed I would never have come here, I am in the practice here and expect to Continue so long as I remain[.] I have control of some mining Claims, upon which I have hands at work, and from which I confidently hope to realize my share within 12 months. I can do a business amounting to at least 8000$ in a year, but probably could not collect more than one half, if that. There are so many destitute Creatures that you Can't make it Come out right[.] You know enough about California times to see the picture, without sketching it any further. So matters wag on here.

Times in Cal are and have been unusually hard. The very dry winter — the Bank failures — the attending swindling operations and Consequent scarcity of coin, make the past few months very hard on the natives of this goodly region.[1] From what you tell me, I suppose that money matters are very stringent throughout the States and will probably remain so for some time. Times here will soon react I think, and business will go on lively again. From my business I manage to get enough to live *well* and keep up my mining interests, which is no small

---

[1] Wayman alludes to the failure of a number of leading banks near the end of February, 1855. Among them were Page, Bacon and Company, and Adams and Company, which had branch offices throughout all the mining areas. See Robert G. Cleland, *History of California, the American Period*, pp. 291–92.

item in the way of expences. I like this portion of Cal as well or better than any I have yet seen[.] The face of the country is much rougher than in and about Shaws Flat, the mountains are higher, Sharper and steeper, Consequently prospecting is more expensieve[.] It is not uncommon for tunnels to be run into the hills, through the bed rock, from 3 to 7 hundred feet before pay dirt is found. Most of the mining done in this district is of this kind. True many of the Gulches, Ravines and banks pay well for Sluicing, but not as a general thing[.] I would give you a description of this region if I tho't it would inter[e]st any of you. I Can't think of any [thing] interesting to say to you, Consequently I will close[.] Tell, Mother that she need not be any uneasy about me, I will take good Care of my self and Come home in due time[.] I would be much pleased to see you all this Spring, but I think that you all will agree with me, when I tell you that I have not yet Completed my mission, and must stay a while longer. Say to Juliet that I think she is quite young to leave home, but go on. I would be pleased to hear from our New Castle folks. You will please write me by return mail and tell me every thing, you Can think of, and I will be ready to respond, more at length. My best wishes, and Compliments to all, each and everyone of you, individually and collectively[.] I will say again write *very soon* and oblige[.]

J. H. Wayman

PS.
Direct your letters to Forest City Sierra Co Cal[.]
We have a Post office here now[.]

\* \* \*

Forest City California<br>June 11th 1855

Bro J. V. Wayman,

I answered yours of March 4th and again am writing you without any thing in Return. I would have written you two weeks ago, but the Mail Closed before I thought of it. My object in writing now is to give you an item in regard to a notion I have had, and still have of paying a visit to *Guaymas,* Sonora Mexico. The place is situated in Latitude 28° a most beautiful Climate — one Eternal spring amonge all the Tropical fruits in full perfection. The time is not far off when this portion of Mexico will belong to Uncle Sam, and when that time does arrive Guaymas will make one of the most desireable locations for private life, on the American Continent[.] I will probably remain in my present location until next Spring. If I Conclude not to do so, I will give you notice in due time. My present notion is, that I will visit home next Spring[1] by way of Guaymas, if I don't Conclude to spend the Coming winter there. My opinion is, that the next Congress will complete the work that is now pending in regard to the

---
[1] Following *spring* Wayman crossed out *going*.

purchase of Sonora if it should, *that is* the place of all places according to my way of thinking[.] Sebastopal *not* yet taken,[2] I have just read the news from the States of May 12th giving an outline of the Condition of things before Sebastopol. (*It suits me*) I have readily Come to the Conclusion that the Allies[3] are about used up, and are only now seeking some excuse to raise the Siege — Austria now occupies the attitude before the world that she always did at heart, I always thought it *very* strange that Austria Should join the Allies —

If Austria and Prussia act at all, they will be with Russia, in such an event, as this, the Combined powers of Europe never Can bring them to any other than their own terms of peace. The Vienna Conference[4] like every other act touching the war, has resulted to the disadvantage of the Allies[.] Russia made the Conference answer the end that she intended it should from the first, Amonge which was to neutralize Austria, and to gain time, which is as disasterous to the Allies as defeat in the field of battle would be.

I have not yet heard one word from one of the tribe save your self, Since my residence in this region. I would Certainly like to hear from all of you often — I would write you more at length if I had any grounds to go upon — Say to Bros Wm & Milton that I would write them, but I have exhausted my news bag and Can't write until I hear from them.

If I had any excuse to do so, I would write you every mail. I always feel so d—d mad when my letters remain unanswered that I Can't say what I would say in a decent manner.

Well, write very soon & tell me of our folks in New Castle[.] Say to Juliet that I have waited for an answer to my letter, as long as she had to wait on my negligence, Consequently I will now look for some word soon[.]

   PS   You will Send yo[u]r word direct to Forest City
                                    Sierra Co Cal

I would like to say more — *but Can't at present*[.]

                                            *J. H. Wayman*

---

[2] After England and France declared war on Russia in March, 1854, Sebastopol was the object of a great siege, which lasted for nearly a year. The fortress fell in September, 1855.
[3] England, France, and Turkey. Austria and Prussia also formed an alliance to oppose Russia.
[4] This conference set down conditions of peace with Russia. The terms were rejected.

# LETTERS

Forest City August 2nd 1858[1]

Bro J. V. Wayman

Your word was received last evening, and I hasten to reply, It seems that you are doomed to be annoyed, belied, beset and beleaguered by a set of low Curs, long as you remain in Cambridge, After duly considering all the attending circumstances and etceteras, I would much prefer that you remain and see the whole matter settled.— It would be much better for your family and yourself[.] To leave the country under existing circumstances, would forever leave a stain that would remain during the memory of the conditions that first called it into existance. In regard to said "rape"!! *Good God!!* one-*Hell of a rape!!* Such stuff is rediculously absurb. I know nothing of her myself other than what common rumor said. The letter of which you speak, written to Jim Hunt, contained nothing more than the common gossip at the time —

Damn it, every body knew of her operations,— of her many seductions,— and[2] numerous *"rapes' without "Chloroform."*[3] I wonder if Joab Lawrence was under the necessity of *giving* her "Chloroform"! if so, I presume he must have used up a damned large quantity, considering the circumstances in a *numerical* point of view.

As to myself, I have only to say, that I am now making my arrang[e]ments to leave the mountains next Spring for good, And am strongly in favor of San Francisco for a location,— But, before I make any definite arrangements, I will see you, I must and will visit you in the Spring[.]

The *Frazer river* excitement[4] in California, has nearly ruined many mining towns, and F City among the number, I have been largely looser by so many dishonest creatures leaving without paying, I am now determined to play for even as near as I can, and quit the game in these *"diggings"*[.] I can command a business here (if I could collect it) worth 10,000$ easy in one year, but it is a damned poor consolation to know that you can do all this, without[5] half pay. This seems to be the general tendency of all business in the mountains at

---

[1] Written in ink in the upper right corner are the following: *W G W*, *Wayman W G*, and *W G Wayman*. *Forest* is written in ink below *Forest City*. The remainder of the manuscript is in pencil. The additions in ink were apparently made by Wayman's nephew, Willard G. Wayman, the only member of the family who had the initials *W. G. W.*

[2] Wayman crossed out *of* following *and*.

[3] *Enough of this* is crossed out following *chloroform*.

[4] Wayman here refers to the discovery of gold in 1857 along the Fraser River in British Columbia. Exaggerated reports of rich gold deposits led to a boom which induced many miners to leave California gold camps during the following spring. See Ray Allen Billington, *Far Western Frontier*, pp. 244–48.

[5] Wayman struck out *more than* following *without*.

present, I suppose that *Captain Jim*[6] [Sim?] and satellites, have been concocting, studying and brooding over this damned annoyance, in secrete conclave, for some time; and now that their favorite is *being born,* they will be forced to call the monster by it's legitimate name ("slander the foulest whelp of sin")[7] to keep the family relationship up[.] Such demonstrations are but the sickly efforts of a low and sordid mind, only fit by nature and habit, to consort with the *envious, low* and *vulgar.*

I will be with you in the spring, or sooner if it should become necessary, and I *pledge* you my word, I *will cowhide* any damned son of a Bitch that gives me a lawful excuse, and I will be the judge of the excuse myself. Enough of this, I feel a little better now. I am pleased to hear of Betsey and family doing well, and Bro Milton still converting *damned sinners.* Tell Elizabeth[8] to write me. I have not heard from her direct for some years. I presume that Milton is too busy[9] in his labors of saving sinners, to write me; consequently he is *excused.* Is Milton a Black Republican yet? I hope not, if he is, I don't wish to know it. I have no sympathy — no feeling — no respect for such. I think them, *mean and dishonest.*

If there is any necessity for it, I will send money enough to meet the demand against my house — you will let me know the amount, and all about it. I don't think any thing of the property, but dislike to have the damned brutes having to do with any thing belonging to me — Since the fire — Forest City has been built up nicely, indeed looks better than before,[10] but for the *Frazer river* excitement, would have been quite a business burgh. I have my office now furnished again quite respectably. I did not build, because I concluded not to remain longer than spring[.]

I think it would afford me some pleasure to visit Cambridge City again,

---

[6] Wayman may allude to James Douglas (1803–77), chief factor of the Hudson's Bay Company. In order to maintain order and keep the unruly element from California out of his territory, he imposed taxation on all persons wishing to mine along the Fraser River. See Billington, p. 247. If their inference is correct, then Wayman's resentment stemmed from his financial losses as a result of the exodus of miners from the mines near Forest City.

[7] From the poem *The Course of Time* (Edinburgh, 1827), by Robert Pollok (1798–1827), a Scottish poet.

[8] Wayman's sister, born in 1822.

[9] The words *with his* are crossed off following *busy.*

[10] A picture of Forest City as it appeared before this fire, which destroyed the town, is in Hutchings' *Illustrated California Magazine,* II (June, 1858–June, 1859), 104. The fire apparently occurred early in 1858.

Well, I will try it before long. I suppose Willard[11] and Bell[12] are well grown by this time, I would like to see them, How is my namesake?[13]

My best wishes to all, Write me by return mail if you can[.] I will be anxious to learn how times are working[.]

Yours Very Truly<br><br>J. H. Wayman

❋ ❋ ❋

Carson City [Nevada] March 25th 1862

Bro J. V. Wayman.

Your word was duly received and would have been answered sooner — but for an attack of Rheumatism which annoyed me three weeks or more — I am now myself again, and am seated to tell a small portion of what I could or would say, could I see you in person.

The sad news of Bell's[1] death to me is distressing indeed — She was my favorite among all the relations of our family. I have often determined in my own mind, to pay you a visit and (with your permission) bring Bell with me to this country. It seems to me, that, I can't cherish a hope ever, without some disaster lurking around to mar or destroy all that is pleasant or desireable in life.

Since I saw you last, time has made sad havoc in our family,— And you, and I, will ere-long be called hence. "So mote it be" I am *always ready*.

I am pleased to learn, that Willard[2] is making manly strides towards the Completion of his professional studies, When he graduates, I would like very well to have him Come to this Country, and do business with me. A fine field is open here, and I can give him plenty to do — What say you?

The present distracted Condition of our Country,[3] is lamentable indeed,— We have here daily news from the Capitol, as well as the Army movements in different quarters, all of which is unreliable, *worse, dam–d lies,* which will require a long time to set right, if ever. History will never be able to give a true picture of the now-passing events.

*Abe* and his Abolition hordes will ere long, find themselves in the wrong pew, when the wholesome–mandate will be proclaimed "hunt your holes!!"

---

[11] His nephew (born 1839), son of Wayman's brother James.

[12] His niece Isabella (born 1841), daughter of his brother James.

[13] John Vallores Wayman (born 1856), son of his brother James.

---

[1] Isabella, daughter of Wayman's brother James. She died on November 20, 1861.

[2] Son of Wayman's brother James. In 1862 he was 21 years old and a medical student. Later he did go to California, and after his uncle's death became executor of his estate. He married Lizzie Ormsby, daughter of Wayman's wife by her first marriage to Major William Ormsby.

[3] Wayman alludes, of course, to the Civil War.

I have ever looked upon the present[4] unholy onslaught, as being a second edition to the John-Brown forray[5] on a large scale, engendered by the same dishonest motives,— Kept up by the same thirst for gain,— and fed by the Craven menials who ever act by proxey ——— And I *do* hope in God's name, that, the same retributive justice, will be meeted out to[6] Abe, &, Co. as was to his greate prototype or *fore-runner*, "*Ossawottamie Brown.*"[7]

I am in the practice here — plenty to do, but small returns. Times are, and have been during the past winter, very hard — We hope soon to have easy times in money matters.

I want to visit you soon as I can do so without crippling my present arrangements — I will try and come over next fall or winter.

This is evidently the richest portion of God's earth, or will be, when fully developed. (in minerals I mean)[8] I have not heard a word from any of our family but your self, for more than a year — Bro Milton has never written me at all, I don't wish him to write, if he is a *black-Abe* man, as I suspect he is,

Well, I will write you again soon, and give you a full account of myself — I am interested in Several mining claims, in different regions of the Territory,[9] but don't know thier worth yet, but soon will; if they prove to be worth anything, it will be quite an item.

We have in Carson City a Masonic Lodge & an Odd Fellows Lodge —recently organized, and in good order,— this you may not care to know. I am identified with both, which will not be any disadavantage to me at present, as

---

[4] Following *present*, Wayman struck out the word *onslaught*.

[5] Wayman refers to John Brown's seizure of the government arsenal at Harpers Ferry, Virginia, on October 16–17, 1859, and probably to his violent abolitionist activities in Kansas in 1856 as well.

[6] *Them* is crossed out after *to*.

[7] In August, 1856, at Osawatomie, Kansas, Brown stood off a raid of proslavery elements from Missouri.

[8] The Comstock Lode had been discovered in 1859 at Virginia City, and further discoveries were made in Esmeraldo and Humboldt counties. Wayman's opinion that this was "the richest portion of God's earth" was quite true, for the Comstock Lode, which was 300 feet wide, proved to be one of the greatest mining discoveries in the history of the country. Within twenty years it produced $300,000,000 in precious metals. The influx of California miners into Nevada after 1858 and the rapid development of the area had probably been responsible for Wayman's decision to leave Forest City and move to Nevada himself. A good account of the Comstock Lode is in Rodman W. Paul, *Mining Frontiers of the Far West, 1848–1880*, pp. 56–86.

[9] Nevada Territory, as it was known after the division of Utah Territory in 1861 into two parts.

you know all new Lodges are better patronized than old ones. I am a *Knight-Templer* in Masonry— You will please answer soon as Convenient and I will give you a full history of this Territory and my doings therein—

My best wishes to all while I remain

Very Truly Yours

J. H. Wayman

P.S  I am half promised to marry next fall, but have not fully made up my mind yet. If I do, it will be Kentucky-stock of the Trumbo tribe.[10] You may know them[.]

---

[10] A certificate of marriage in the Ormsby County courthouse at Carson City, Nevada, shows that he married Margaret A. (Trumbo) Ormsby here in February, 1863. The marriage ceremony was performed by Orion Clemens, then serving as governor in the absence of Governor James W. Nye. Mrs. Ormsby was the widow of Major William Ormsby, who was killed by Indians at Pyramid Lake in May, 1860. See also introduction, pp. 17–18.

# Bibliography

## MANUSCRIPTS

ANABLE, HENRY SHELDON. Journal. From Sheboygan, Wisconsin, to Sacramento, California, in the year of 1852. Transcript. Huntington Library.

ASHLEY, MRS. ALGELINE JACKSON. Diary of Mrs. Algeline Jackson Ashley in 1852. Transcript. Huntington Library.

BAKER, WILLIAM P. Diary. March 12, 1852–. Transcript. California State Library.

BAILEY, MARY STUART. A journal of Mary Stuart Bailey, wife of Dr. Fred Bailey, from Ohio to Cal[ifornia], April–October, 1852. Huntington Library.

BRIGGS, ROBERT. [Biographical Sketches. *ca.* 1887]. To California from Missouri, 1852. . . . Bancroft Library.

BRUCE, RACHEL C. [Rachel C. Rose] Diary. March 24, 1852–Aug. 18, 1852. Bancroft Library.

CALLISON, JOHN JOSEPH. The Diary of John Joseph Callison; Oregon Trail, 1852. Reproduced by the Lane County Pioneer-Historical Society, Eugene, Oregon, 1958. Transcript. California Historical Society.

CRANE, A[DDISON] M[OSES]. Journal of a trip across the plains in 1852, March 26–August 28. Huntington Library.

DAUGHTERS, J. M. Journal, describing trip across the plains in 1852, from Indiana to the crossing of the Truckee River. March 14, 1852, to August 14, 1852. Negative photostat. California State Library.

EGBERT, MRS. ELIZA ANN (MCAULEY). Diary of Mrs. Eliza Ann Egbert. A record of a journey across the Plains in '52. Transcript. California Historical Society.

FINLEY, NEWTON GLEAVES. Memories of travel [across the plains in 1852]. Transcript. Bancroft Library.

FOX, JARED. Memorandum kept from Dellton, Sauk Co., Wisconsin towards California & Oregon. April 1852–. Transcript. Bancroft Library.

GRAHAM, ALPHEUS N. Journal kept by Alpheus N. Graham from Coles County, Illinois, to California in the Year 1852. Transcript. California State Library.

HANNA, ESTHER BELLE. Diary of a Journey from Pittsburg to Oregon City, March 11–December 20, 1852. Transcript. Bancroft Library.

HAWLEY, A. H. Lake Tahoe. San Francisco, 1883. To California in 1852 via Carson Valley; remarks on John Reese's Mormon Station and on Lucky Bill Thorrington's trading post. . . . Bancroft Library.

125

HICKMAN, PETER L. Diary, 1852–1856. Transcript. California State Library.

JONES, EVAN O. Diary, 1852. Bancroft Library.

KEEGAN, ELIZABETH J. C. Letter to James and Julia Keegan from Sacramento, Dec. 12, 1852. Transcript. California Historical Society.

KNAPP, JABEZ B. Letter to David R. Sessions, Portland, Oregon, 1889. (Emigration to Oregon, 1852.) Bancroft Library.

KNOTT, THOMAS. Personal Rem[iniscences]. 1881. Photocopy. (To California from Michigan, 1852. . . .) Bancroft Library.

LEWIS, JOHN N. Diary of an Overland Journey to Oregon 1851–1855 [1852]. Bancroft Library.

MCKINSTRY, BYRON NATHAN. California Gold Rush Diary, 1850–1852. Photocopy of transcript with explanatory notes. Bancroft Library.

MANN, STEPHEN H[ODGE]. Family papers, 1848–1937. Bancroft Library.

MAPEL, ELI B. [Account of experiences crossing the plains from Iowa, 1852, and pioneering in Washington Territory. 1876.] Bancroft Library.

MASON, NATHANIEL HOCKET ALLAN. Statement [188–?]. Bancroft Library.

MEISTER, JOHN. Diary. (In German.) California State Library.

MILLER, SILAS V. Letter to his brother. Salem, Oregon, Nov. 24, 1852. Negative photocopy. Bancroft Library.

PADEN, WILLIAM G. Set of Township Maps (blueprints). Bancroft Library.

RICHARDSON, ALPHEUS. Diary . . . 1852–1853. Transcript. Bancroft Library.

RICHARDSON, CAROLINE L. Journal and commonplace-book. 1852–53? Bancroft Library.

ROSE, RACHEL C. See Rachel C. Bruce.

RUDD, LYDIA A[LLEN (Morrison)]. [Diary of Overland Journey from St. Joseph, Mo., to Burlington, Oregon. . . . May 6–Oct. 27, 1852.] Huntington Library.

SAWYER, MRS. FRANCIS H. Overland to California; notes from a journal kept by Mrs. Francis H. Sawyer on a journey across the plains [Ap. 25]–Aug. 17, 1852. Transcript. Bancroft Library.

SMITH, ASA and SETH. Letters 1850–1862. Written from California gold fields to family in Baltimore. Bancroft Library.

SMITH, G. A. Diary. April 15–July 16, 1852. Film. (Original manuscript is at the Missouri Historical Society.) Bancroft Library.

TAYLOR, WILLIAM. [Remininscences.] 1884. Recollections of overland journeys to California, 1852 and 1853. Film. Bancroft Library.

VERDENAL, JOHN M., and DOMINIQUE VERDENAL. Journal . . . from St. Louis, Mo., to Placerville by Land, 1852. Transcript. Bancroft Library.

ZINN, HENRY, SR. Records of Henry Zinn, Sr., pertaining to trip to California. Diary of an 1852 trip to California by Henry Zinn, Sr., from St. Joseph, Missouri, to Eureka City, Sierra County, California. California State Library.

## BOOKS

ALLEN, ELEANOR. *Canvas Caravans . . . Based on the Journal of Esther Belle McMillen Hanna, Who, with Her Husband, Rev. Joseph A. Hanna, Brought the Presbyterian Colony to Oregon in 1852.* Portland, Oregon: Binfords & Mort, 1946.

BAUGHMAN, ROBERT W. *Kansas in Maps.* Topeka: The Kansas State Historical Society, 1961.

BAUR, JOHN E. "The Health Factor in the Gold Rush Era," in *Rushing for Gold*, ed. John Walton Caughey. Berkeley and Los Angeles: University of California Press, 1949.

# BIBLIOGRAPHY

BILLINGTON, RAY ALLEN. *The Far Western Frontier, 1830–1860.* New York: Harper & Brothers, 1956.

BRUFF, J. GOLDSBOROUGH. *Gold Rush. The Journals, Drawings, and other Papers of J. Goldsborough Bruff,* eds. Georgia Willis Read and Ruth Gaines. California Centennial Edition. New York: Columbia University Press, 1949.

BURT, WILLIAM H., and RICHARD P. GROSSENHEIDER. *A Field Guide to the Mammals.* Boston: Houghton Mifflin Co., 1964.

CARSON, J[AMES] H. *Early Recollections of the Mines, and a Description of the Great Tulare Valley.* Stockton: Published to accompany the steamer edition of the "San Joaquin Republican," 1852.

CAUGHEY, JOHN WALTON. *Gold is the Cornerstone.* Berkeley and Los Angeles: University of California Press, 1948.

CHAPPELL, PHIL. E. "A History of the Missouri River." *Transactions of the Kansas State Historical Society, 1905–1906.* Vol. IX. Topeka: State Printing Office, 1906.

CHILD, ANDREW. *Overland Route to California; Description of the Route, via Council Bluffs, Iowa. . . .* Introduction by Lyle H. Wright. Los Angeles: N. A. Kovach, 1946. (Originally published in Milwaukee by the Daily Sentinel Steam Power Press, 1852.)

CLARK, JOHN HAWKINS. *Overland to the Gold Fields in 1852: the Journal of John Hawkins Clark, Expanded & Revised from Notes Made During the Journey,* ed. Louise Barry. Topeka: Kansas State Printing Plant, 1942.

CLELAND, ROBERT G. *History of California: The American Period.* New York: The Macmillan Co., 1922.

CLEMENS, SAMUEL L. See Mark Twain.

COOKE, LUCY RUTLEDGE. *Crossing the Plains in 1852. Narrative of a Trip from Iowa to "The Land of Gold" as Told in Letters Written during the Journey.* Modesto, California: Privately Printed, 1923.

CRAWFORD, CHARLES HOWARD. *Scenes of Earlier Days in Crossing the Plains to Oregon, and Experiences of Western Life.* Petaluma, California, 1898; reprinted Chicago: Quadrangle Books, Inc., 1962.

DELANO, ALONZO. *Across the Plains and Among the Diggings.* New York: Wilson-Erickson, Inc., 1936.

DE SMET, P. J. *Letters and Sketches: with a Narrative of a Year's Residence Among the Indian Tribes of the Rocky Mountains* (Philadelphia, 1843). Reprinted in *Early Western Travels,* ed. R. G. Thwaites. Cleveland: The Arthur H. Clark Co., 1904. Vol. XXVII.

*Dictionary of American Biography,* ed. Dumas Malone. 22 vols. New York: Charles Scribner's Sons, 1932.

DUNLOP, RICHARD. *Doctors of the American Frontier.* New York: Doubleday & Co., Inc., 1965.

ELLISON, ROBERT SPURRIER. *Independence Rock, the Great Record of the Desert.* Casper, Wyoming: Natrona County Historical Society, 1930.

FERGUSON, DELANCEY. *Mark Twain: Man and Legend.* New York: The Bobbs-Merrill Co., 1953.

FOSTER, MRS. ROXANA (CHENEY). *The Foster Family, California Pioneers.* Santa Barbara: Schauer Printing Studio, Inc., 1925.

FRIZZELL, LODISA. *Across the Plains to California in 1852; Journal of Mrs. Lodisa Frizzell,* ed. Victor H. Paltsits. New York: The New York Public Library, 1915.

GAY, THERESSA. *James Marshall, the Discoverer of California Gold. A Biography.* Georgetown. California: The Talisman Press, 1967.

GREEN, JAY. *Diary of Jay Green, Covering the Period May, 1852, to July 27, 1852, During the Crossing of the Plains & Mountains in a Journey from Duncan's Ferry, Mo., to Hangtown*

(*Placerville*), *Calif.*, ed. Merrell Kitchen. Stockton: San Joaquin Pioneer & Historical Society, n.d.

GROH, GEORGE W. *Gold Fever: Being a True Account, both Horrifying and Hilarious, of the Art of Healing (so-called) During the California Gold Rush.* New York: William Morrow & Co., Inc., 1966.

GUDDE, ERIVEN G. *California Place Names.* Berkeley: University of California Press, 1962.

HAFEN, LEROY R., and FRANCIS M. YOUNG. *Fort Laramie and the Pageant of the West, 1834–1890.* Glendale: Arthur H. Clark Co., 1938.

HANNA, PHIL TOWNSEND (comp.). *The Dictionary of California Land Names.* Rev. Los Angeles: The Automobile Club of Southern California, 1951.

HARRIS, HENRY. *California's Medical Story.* San Francisco: J. W. Stacey, Inc., 1932.

HICKMAN, RICHARD. *An Overland Journey to California in 1852: the Journal of Richard Owen Hickman*, ed. M. Catherine White. Missoula: State University of Montana, 1929.

HIEB, DAVID L. *Fort Laramie National Monument.* National Park Service Historical Handbook Series No. 20. Washington, D.C., 1954.

*History of Wayne County.* Interstate Publishing Company, 1884.

HITTEL, JOHN S. *The Resources of California, Comprising Agriculture, Mining, Geography, Climate, Commerce.* . . . San Francisco: A. Roman & Co.; New York: W. J. Widdleton, 1863.

HORN, HOSEA B. *Horn's Overland Guide from . . . Council Bluffs . . . to Sacramento.* New York: J. H. Colton, 1852.

*Hutching's Illustrated California Magazine.* Vol. III (July, 1858, to June, 1859). San Francisco: Hutchings & Rosenfield, Publishers, 1859.

*Illustrated History of Plumas, Lassen & Sierra Counties, with California from 1513 to 1850.* San Francisco: Faris & Smith, 1882.

IRVING, WASHINGTON. *The Adventures of Captain Bonneville*, ed. Edgeley W. Todd. Norman: University of Oklahoma Press, 1961.

———. *Astoria; or, Anecdotes of an Enterprise Beyond the Rocky Mountains*, ed. Edgeley W. Todd. Norman: University of Oklahoma Press, 1964.

JONES, J. ROY. *Memories, Men and Medicine. A History of Medicine in Sacramento, California.* Sacramento: Sacramento Society for Medical Improvement, 1950.

KELLY, J. WELLS. *First Directory of Nevada Territory, Containing the Names of Residents in the Principal Towns.* . . . San Francisco: Valentine & Co., 1862.

KETT, JOSEPH F. *The Formation of the American Medical Profession.* New Haven and London: Yale University Press, 1968.

KNIGHT, WILLIAM HENRY. [Scrapbooks compiled for the Handbook Almanac for the Pacific States, edited by W. H. Knight and Published by H. H. Bancroft, 1862–1864.] 40 vols.

KOENIG, GEORGE. *Ghosts of the Gold Rush, being a Wayward Guide to the Mother Lode Country.* Glendale, California: La Siesta Press, 1968.

[LETTS, J. M.] *California Illustrated: Including a Description of the Panama and Nicaragua Routes.* By a Returned Californian. New York: William Holdredge, Publisher, 1852.

MACK, EFFIE MONA. *Mark Twain in Nevada.* New York: Charles Scribner's Sons, 1947.

MARCY, RANDOLPH. *The Prairie Traveler. A Hand-book for Overland Expeditions.* New York: Harper & Brothers, Publishers, 1859.

MATTES, MERRILL J. *Scotts Bluff National Monument.* National Park Service Historical Handbook Series No. 28. Washington, D.C., 1958.

## BIBLIOGRAPHY

MEEKER, EZRA. *The Ox Team; or, The Old Oregon Trail, 1852–1906.* . . . 4th ed. New York: The author, 1907.

MONAGHAN, JAMES. *The Overland Trail.* Indianapolis: Bobbs-Merrill Co., 1947.

MORGAN, DALE. *Guide to the California Manuscripts in the Bancroft Library.* 10 vols. (typescript).

MORGAN, DALE L. and GEORGE P. HAMMOND (eds.). *A Guide to the Manuscript Collections of the Bancroft Library.* Berkeley and Los Angeles: University of California Press, 1963. Vol. I: Pacific and Western Manuscripts (except California).

MYERS, BURTON D. *The History of Medical Education in Indiana.* Bloomington: Indiana University Press, 1956.

NADEAU, REMI. *Fort Laramie and the Sioux Indians.* Englewood Cliffs, N.J.: Prentice-Hall, Inc., 1967.

———. *Ghost Towns and Mining Camps of California.* Los Angeles: The Ward Ritchie Press, 1965.

PACKARD, FRANCIS R. *History of Medicine in the United States.* 2 v. New York and London: Hafner Publishing Co., 1963.

PADEN, IRENE D. *The Wake of the Prairie Schooner.* New York: The Macmillan Co., 1944.

PADEN, WILLIAM G. Photographs of the Oregon Trail. 26 mounted photographs. Unpublished. Bancroft Library.

PARKER, REV. SAMUEL. *Journal of an Exploring Tour Beyond the Rocky Mountains.* 3rd ed. Ithaca, N.Y.: Mack, Andrus, & Woodruff, 1842.

PAUL, RODMAN W. *California Gold. The Beginnings of Mining in the Far West.* Cambridge: Harvard University Press, 1947.

———. *Mining Frontiers of the Far West, 1848–1880.* New York: Holt, Rinehart and Winston, 1963.

PERKINS, ELISHA DOUGLASS. *Gold Rush Diary. Being the Journal of Elisha Douglass Perkins on the Overland Trail in the Spring and Summer of 1849,* ed. Thomas D. Clark. Lexington: University of Kentucky Press, 1967.

PLATT, P. L. and N. SLATER. *Travelers' Guide Across the Plains upon the Overland Route to California.* Introduction by Dale Morgan. San Francisco: John Howell, 1963. A reprint of the original edition published in Chicago in 1852.

PRITCHARD, JAMES A. *The Overland Diary of James A. Pritchard from Kentucky to California in 1849,* ed. Dale L. Morgan. Denver: The Old West Publishing Company, 1959.

PRUCHA, FRANCIS PAUL. *A Guide to the Military Posts of the United States, 1789–1895.* Madison: The State Historical Society of Wisconsin, 1964.

*Route of the Oregon Trail in Idaho.* Boise: Idaho Department of Highways, 1963, 1967.

SHINN, CHARLES HOWARD. *Mining Camps. A Study in American Frontier Government.* New York: Charles Scribner's Sons, 1885.

STABAEK, TOSTEN KITTELSON. *An Account of a Journey to California in 1852.* Northfield, Minnesota: Studies and Records, 1929.

STANSBURY, HOWARD. *An Expedition to the Valley of the Great Salt Lake of Utah.* Philadelphia: Lippincott, Grambo, and Co., 1852.

STEWART, GEORGE R. *The California Trail: an Epic with Many Heroes.* American Trails Series. New York: McGraw-Hill Book Co., Inc., 1962.

THOMAS, MELVIN R. "The Impact of the California Gold Rush on Ohio and Ohioans." Master's Thesis, Ohio State University, 1949.

Thornbrough, Emma Lou. *Indiana in the Civil War Era, 1850–1880*. Indianapolis: Indiana Historical Bureau & Indiana Historical Society, 1965.

Torrence, C. W. *History of Masonry in Nevada*. Reno: A. Carlisle and Co., 1944.

Turnbull, T[homas]. *Travels from the United States Across the Plains to California*. Proceedings of the State Historical Society of Wisconsin, 1913. Madison: Published for the Society, 1914.

Twain, Mark. *Roughing It*. Hillcrest Edition, Vols. VII–VIII. Hartford: The American Publishing Company, 1903.

Ware, Joseph E. *The Emigrants' Guide to California*. St. Louis: J. Halsall, 1849. Reprinted Princeton: Princeton University Press, 1932.

Watson, Estelle Clark. *Some Martin, Jefferies and Wayman Families and Connections of Virginia, Kentucky, and Indiana*. Skokie, Ill.: Guild Press, Inc., 1965.

Wheat, Carl Irving. *Books of the California Gold Rush, a Centennial Selection*. San Francisco: The Colt Press, 1949.

_____. *The Maps of the California Gold Region, 1848–1857. A Bibliocartography of an Important Decade*. San Francisco: The Grabhorn Press, 1942.

Wilkins, James F. *An Artist on the Overland Trail. The 1849 Diary and Sketches of James F. Wilkins*, ed. John Francis McDermott. San Marino: The Huntington Library, 1968.

Wyman, Walker D. "The Outfitting Posts," in *Rushing for Gold*, ed. John Walton Caughey. Berkeley and Los Angeles: University of California Press, 1949.

## PERIODICALS

Adams, Cecelia Emily McMillen. "Crossing the Plains in 1852." *Transactions of the Thirty-second Annual Reunion of the Oregon Pioneer Association for 1904*. Portland, 1905.

Akin, James, Jr. "The Journal of James Akin, Jr.," ed. Edward Everett Dale. *University of Oklahoma Bulletin*. New Series No. 172. University Studies No. 9. Norman, Oklahoma, June 1, 1919.

Bagley, Clarence B. "Crossing the Plains," *Washington Historical Quarterly*, XIII (July, 1922), 163–180.

Bieber, Ralph P. "California Gold Mania," *Mississippi Valley Historical Review*, XXXV (June, 1948), 3–28.

Clark, John Hawkins. "Overland to the Gold Fields of California in 1852. The Journal of John Hawkins Clark, Expanded and Revised from Notes Made During the Journey," ed. Louise Barry. *Kansas Historical Quarterly*, XI (Aug., 1942), 227–296.

Conyers, E. W. "Diary of E. W. Conyers, a Pioneer of 1852." *Transactions of the Thirty-Third Annual Reunion of the Oregon Pioneer Association*. Portland, 1906.

Harris, Earl R. "Courthouse and Jail Rocks, Landmarks on the Oregon Trail," *Nebraska History*, XXXXIII (March, 1962), 29–51.

Inman, Margaret Windsor. "My Arrival in Washington in 1852," *Washington Historical Quarterly*, XVIII (October, 1927), 254–260.

Kerns, John T. "Journal of Crossing the Plains to Oregon in 1852." *Transactions of the Forty-Second Annual Reunion of the Oregon Pioneer Association*. Portland, 1917.

McAllister, Rev. John. "Diary of Rev. John McAllister, a Pioneer of 1852." *Transactions of the Fiftieth Annual Reunion of the Oregon Pioneer Association*. Portland, 1925.

## BIBLIOGRAPHY

MANTOR, LYLE E. "Fort Kearny and the Westward Movement," *Nebraska History,* XXIX (Sept., 1948), 175–207.

MATTES, MERRILL J. "Chimney Rock on the Oregon Trail," *Nebraska History,* XXXVI (March, 1955), 1–26.

———. "Hiram Scott, Fur Trader," *Nebraska History,* XXVI (Sept., 1945), 127–162.

[Forest City, California.] *Quarterly of the Society of California Pioneers,* VI (Dec., 1929), 183.

READ, GEORGIA WILLIS. "Diseases, Drugs, and Doctors on the Oregon-California Trail in the Gold-Rush Years," *Missouri Historical Review,* XXXVIII (April, 1944), 260–276.

SUDWEEKS, LESLIE L. "The Raft River in Idaho History," *Pacific Northwest Quarterly,* XXXII (July, 1941), 289–305.

WILLMAN, LILLIAN M. "The History of Fort Kearney," *Publications of the Nebraska Historical Society,* XXI (1930), 213–326.

# Index

Ale–Nease Creek: 32 & n.
Alexander Crater: 66 & n.
American River: 1, 88
Anable, Henry S.: quoted, 29n.
Arbon Valley: 68n.
Ash Hollow: 40 & n.
Ashlie Creek: 63, 65n.

Bailey, Mary Stuart: quoted, 28n., 35n., 47n., 48n., 83n., 86nn.
Balsey, Leo (Leon): executed for murder, 15, 59n.
Balsley, L.: see Leo Balsey
Bancroft, Hubert H.: quoted, 2
Bannock River: 67n.
Beal (Beel), Mathias: murdered, 15, 59n.
Bear River: 10, 59n., 61n., 62 & n.
Bear River Valley: described, 63
Beer Springs: 65, see also Soda Springs
Bentley, Colonel: 84
Big Blue River: 10, 31 & n.
Big Rock Springs: 68n.
Big Sandy River: 10, 56 & nn., 57n.
Big Vermilion River: 31n.
Bloomfield, J. T.: 115
Boman, G. W.: 96 & n.
Boonville, Mo.: 28 & n.
Bridger, James: 44n.
Brown, John: 122 & n.
Bruce, Rachel C.: quoted, 82nn.
Brush Creek: 73n.
Butler, Doctor: 16, 95

California, travel to: 2, 5; equipment and supplies, 9–10 & n.; numbers on road, 11 & n.; violence, 14–15
Cambridge City, Ind.: 8, 27 & n., 76, 111, 115, 119, 120
Camp Creek: 87n.

Campbell, Maston: 8, cook for Wayman party, 113
Carson City, Nev.: 19, 22n.; Wayman's residence there, 111
Carson Pass: 11, 83n., 85n.; difficulties in crossing, 86n.
Carson River: 11, 79n., 80n., 85n.
Carson Valley: 81, 85
Cassia Creek: 69n., 70n.
Cedar Bluff: 39n.
Chimney Rock: 10, 43 & n.
Cholera: see disease
Cincinnati College Medical School: 4 & n.
Cincinnati, O.: 27, 112
Circle Creek: 70n.
City of Rocks: 11, 70n.
Civil War: 121 & n.
Clark, John H.: quoted, 8, 16, 28n., 29n., 30n., 31n., 34n., 38n.
Cleland, Robert Glass: quoted, 5
Clemens, Orion: 19, 22n., 123n.
Clemens, Samuel: see Mark Twain
Cokeville Butte: 61n., 63n.
Cold Springs: 87 & n.
Cold Spring Creek: 74
Columbia, Calif.: 16, 91 & n., 92, 108
Commissary Ridge: 58n., 59n.
Comstock Lode: 19, 122n.
Conyers, Enoch: quoted, 52n., 57n.
Cooke, Lucy R.: quoted, 46n.
Cooper, William H.: 16, 95 & n.
Cotton Wood Creek: 32
Council Bluffs: 113
Courthouse Rock: 10, 41, 42n., 43 & n.
Crane, A. M.: quoted, 12, 30n., 32n., 33n., 46n., 55n., 74n.

Dairy Creek: 67n.
Deep Creek: 68n.

133

Deep Creek Mountains: 68n.
Delano, Alonzo: quoted, 2, 40n., 43n.
Dempsey Creek: 67n.
De Smet, Father Pierre–Jean: 52n.
Devil's Gate: 52, 53n.
Disease: 5, 12 & n., 13, 14, 60, 69, 82, 99; cholera, 5, 12 & n., 13, 69
Downiesville, Calif.: 22n.

EGLESTON: Wayman tends, 69
Emigrant Springs: 58n.

FARNHAM, ELIJAH B.: quoted, 71n.
Fish Creek: 66n., 67n.
Forest City, Calif.: 18, 19, 22n., 111, 114, 120 & n.
Fort Bridger: 61n.
Fort Hall: 66 & nn.
Fort Kearny: 11n., 34; described, 35n.
Fort Laramie: 10, 41, 45 & n., 46; described, 46nn.
Fox, Jared: 50n., 59n.; quoted, 13, 34n., 38n., 51n., 60n., 61n.
Frozen River: 119 & n., 120
Frémont, John C.: 51n.
Frizzell, Lodisa: 52n., 54n.; quoted, 28n., 29n., 35n., 50nn., 55n.

GOOSE CREEK: 70 & n., 71n.
Goose Creek Mountains: 11, 70 & n.
Goose Creek Valley: 70
Graham, Alpheus: 11, 14, 79–80n.; quoted, 13, 15
Granite City: 69–70 & n.; *see also* City of Rocks
Granite Pass: 70n.
Gravel Creek: 67n.
Green, Jay: quoted, 66n., 72n., 73n.
Green River: 10, 56, 57 & n.
Green River Mountains: 58
Gross, Samuel: 3 & n.
Guaymas, Mexico: 117
Guidebooks: 9

HAMILTON, O.: 27 & n.
Ham's Fork: 10, 58, 59nn.
Ham's Fork Plateau: 59n.
Hangtown, Calif.: 11, 16, 87–88 & n., 90; *see also* Placerville, Calif.
Hanna, Esther: 30n.; quoted, 54n., 59n.
Hawn: 30
Henry, Charles: 115
Hickman, Richard O.: quoted, 11, 32n., 37n., 58n., 61n., 72n.
Hildreth's Diggings: 91n.
Horn, Hosea B.: *Horn's Overland Guide . . .*: 53n., 67n.; quoted, 56n., 78n.
Hot Springs Valley: 72 & n., 73
Hudspeth cutoff: 10, 66nn., 69n.
Hudspeth–Meyers cutoff: *see* Hudspeth cutoff

Humboldt Mountains: 71, 73
Humboldt River: 11, 73 & n., 74
Humboldt Sink: 78n., 79
Humboldt Valley: 75
Hunt, James: 92 & n., 113, 119

ICE SLOUGH: 54n.
Independence Rock: 50, 51, 53n.; described, 52n.
Indian Springs: 58n.
Indiana State Medical Association: 4
Indians: 34, 47, 48n., 55, 58, 59n., 60, 62, 65 & n., 70, 71n., 73n., 75–76 & n.
Inman, Margaret: quoted, 14
Iowa Mission: 30n.
Iowa Point: 30

JAIL ROCK: 10, 42n.
Jamestown, Calif.: 16, 93 & n.
Junction Valley: 70n.

KINNEY cutoff: 57nn.

LAFOUNTAIN: 83; Wayman tends, 82 & nn.
Lank, John A.: 91, 92n., 93
Laramie Mountains: 48 & n.
Laramie Peak: 45 & n., 48
Lava Hot Springs: 67nn.
Leek Springs: 86, 87n.
Lewis, John: 55n.; quoted, 60n., 61n.
Lexington, Mo.: 28 & n.
Little Blue River: 32 & n., 33
Little Malad River: 67n.
Little Sandy River: 32, 55n., 56 & n., 57n.
Loring, William: 8, 56, 62, 70, 75, 82, 84

McFEE: 93
McLaughlin, Charles: 115
McPherson: 8, 28, 30n., 39, 56, 62, 96 & n.
Mc Trade (McT.): 70, 91, 92 & n., 96 & n., 98, 112 & n.
Malad River: 67n.
Mapel, E. B.: quoted, 47n., 52n.
Marsh Creek: 67n.
Marsh Creek Valley: 66, 67n.
Marshall, James W.: discovery of gold, 1
Mary's River: 73n.
Marysville, Calif.: 18, 114, 115
Marysville, Kan.: 10, 31n., 32n.
Medical education: 3–4
Meeker, Ezra: 11; quoted, 13
Miller, Silas V.: quoted, 34, 46n.
Mormon Ferry: on North Platte River, 50 & n.; on Green River, 56, 57 & n.

## INDEX

Mormon Station: 82, 83n., 84
Mountain Spring: 70n.
Mountain Spring Creek: 70
Mountain Willow Creek: 66, *see also* Fish Creek
Muddy Creek: 68 & n.

NEMAHA RIVER: 31 & n.
New Castle, Ind.: 115 & n., 118

OAKLAND, CALIF.: 22 & n.
Oregon Town: 30 & n.
Ormsby, Lizzie Jane: 20, 121n.; ward and later wife of Willard Gross Wayman, 22n.
Ormsby, Margaret A. (née Trumbo): marriage to William M. Ormsby, 20; marriage to John Hudson Wayman, 19, 123n.
Ormsby, William M.: 20n., 121n.; killed by Indians, 19–20, 123n.; reinterment, 22n.
Oyster Ridge: 59n.

PACIFIC BUTTE: 55n.
Pacific Creek: 10, 55 & n., 56n.
Pacific Springs: 55n.
Pannock River: 66; *see also* Bannock River
Parker, Samuel: quoted, 43
Pass Lapine: 92, 93n.
Peck, Joseph: Wayman tends, 69
Pine Creek: 85
Placerville, Calif.: *see* Hangtown
Platt, P. L., and N. Slater, *Travelers' Guide Across the Plains* . . . : 9–10, 30n., 31n., 39n., 49n., 50n., 51n., 53n., 60n., 65n., 66n., 85n.; quoted, 10, 29n., 31n., 32n., 33n., 36n., 38–39n., 40n., 45n., 51, 67n., 68n., 70n., 71n., 72n., 78n., 79n., 83n., 87n.
Platte River: 10, 33, 34, 36
Portneuf River: 67n.
Pritchard, James H.: cited, 28n., 52n.

QUAKING ASP SPRING: 68n.

RAFT RIVER: 10, 68, 68n., 69n., 70
Raggtown: 80 & n., 82
Red Lake: 86n.
Richardson, Alpheus: 70n.; quoted, 27n., 57n., 59n.
Richardson, Caroline: 54n., 76n.; quoted, 43–44n., 47n., 78n., 79n., 86n.
Richmond, Ind.: 27 & n.
Rock Creek: 68n.
Rock Spring: 72n.
Rock Springs Creek: 72n.
Rockland Valley: 68n.
Rudd, Lydia: quoted, 30n., 45n.
Rush Valley: 66

SACRAMENTO, CALIF.: 16, 88, 111–12
Saint Joseph, Mo.: 8, 28, 29n., 112
Saint Louis, Mo.: 8, 27 & n., 112
Salt Range: 55n.
*Saluda* (steamer): 28 & n.
San Francisco, Calif.: 20, 111–12, 114, 115
San Joaquin River: 89n., 90n.
Santa Anna, Antonio López de: 114
Sawyer, Mrs. Francis: 65n.; quoted, 62n., 71n., 78n., 87n.
Scott's Bluff: 10, 43, 44 & n.
Scottsbluff, Neb.: 44n.
Shaw's Flat, Calif.: 16, 91, 92 & n., 93, 94, 95, 117
Shearer, M.: 8, 53
Sheep Creek: 63n.
Sheep Rock: 65n.
Sierra Nevada Mountains: 81, 86
Sim: 92, 113, 115 & n.
Slate Creek: 57nn.
Smith, A. J.: 91, 92n.
Smith, G. A.: quoted, 46n., 73n.
Smith's Fork: 61nn., 62 & n.
Soda Springs: 10, 63, 65 & nn; described, 64
Sonora, Calif.: 16, 90 & n., 91, 92, 93, 94, 95, 96
South Pass: 10, 51n., 54 & n., 56
Springfield, Calif.: 16, 92 & n.
Stabaek, Tosten K.: quoted, 70–71nn.
Stanislaus River: 90 & n., 92
Stansbury, Howard: quoted, 40n., 44n.
Station Butte: 61n.
Stewart, George R.: quoted, 15
Stockton, Calif.: 16, 87 & n.
Stony Creek: 31 & n.
Stuart, Robert: 52n.
Sublett Canyon: 67n., 68n.
Sublett Creek: 68n.
Sublette cutoff: 57, 61n.
Sutter's Fort: 88nn.
Sweetwater River: 10, 51 & n., 53

TATE, LAFAYETTE: executed for murder, 15
Thomas Fork: 62, 63n.
Thousand Springs Creek: 72n., 73n.
Thousand Springs Valley: 11, 71
Tjader, A. W.: medical partner of John H. Wayman in Carson City, 19
Tom's Fork: *see* Thomas Fork
Town Creek: 73n.
Trumbo, Margaret: *see* Margaret Ormsby
Tump Range: 59n.
Turnbull, Thomas: 72n.; quoted, 46n., 52n., 59n., 60n., 65n., 72n., 80n., 86nn., 87n.
Twain, Mark: 19, 20n., 22n.

UINTA MOUNTAINS: 55n., 57n.

135

VERDENAL, J. M.: quoted, 13, 15, 72n., 73n., 79n.
Vinton, Elbridge: 8, 27, 96 & n.
Virginia City, Nev.: 122n.

WAYMAN, ELIZABETH (née Clore): 3n., 120 & n.
Wayman, Guy Trumbo: 22n.
Wayman, Herman: 3n.
Wayman, Isabella: 121 & n.
Wayman, James Vallores: 3 & n., 16, 46, 92n., 111
Wayman, John Hudson: 1, 2, 3, 5, 9; parents, 3; medical education, 4; overland route of, 10–11; supplies for travel, 10n.; on diseases of emigrants, 14 (quoted), 60; quoted, 16, 18, 19; begins mining, 18, 99; takes up residence in Forest City, Calif., 18, 114; visits family in Indiana, 18; moves to Carson City, 19; medical partnership with A. W. Tjader, 19; marriage to Margaret A. Ormsby, 19, 123n.; death and burial, 20n., 20–21; invites nephew to join him in medical practice, 22n.; Masonic affiliation, 22n.; reinterment, 22n.; leaves Cambridge City, Ind., 27; his guide, 47, 48n.; patients, 99, Egleston, 69, Joseph Peck, 69, La Fountain, 82 & nn.; Free Masonry, 111; letters to brother James from Indian territory, 112–13; from Forest City, Calif., 114–21, from Carson City, 121–23; in Acapulco, Mexico, 114; in Guaymas, Mexico, 114; in Panama, 114; member Masonic lodge, 122; member of Odd Fellows lodge, 122; as Knight Templar, 123
Wayman, Juliet: 115 & n.; 117, 118
Wayman, Margaret A.: death and burial, 20; reinterment, 22n.; *see also* Margaret Ormsby
Wayman, Milton Herman: 3n., 111, 118, 120, 122
Wayman, Moses (father of John Hudson Wayman): 3 & n.

Wayman overland party: members, 8; begins journey, 9, 30; supplies, 9–10; summary of route, 10–11; disbands at Hangtown, 16; crosses Missouri River and camps, 29–30; reaches Big Blue River, 31; reaches Little Blue River, 32; reaches Platte River, 33; arrives at Fort Kearney, 34; crosses South Platte, 38; reaches Ash Hollow, 40; crosses North Platte, 41; passes Courthouse Rock and Chimney Rock, 43; passes Scott's Bluff, 44; reaches Fort Laramie, 45; leaves North Platte, 50; reaches Sweetwater River, 51; at Independence Rock, 51; camps near Devil's Gate, 52; crosses South Pass, 54–55; camps on Pacific Creek, 55; camps on Little Sandy, 56; crosses Big Sandy, 56; crosses Green River, 56; on Ham's Fork, 56; on Smith's Fork of Bear River, 62; at Soda Springs, 63–65; reaches Portneuf River, 66; camps on Raft River, 68; camps at City of Rocks, 69; camps in Goose Creek Valley, 70; in Thousand Springs Valley, 71; reaches Humboldt River, 73; at Humboldt Sink, 79; reaches Raggtown, 80; crosses Carson Pass, 85–86; at Leek Spring, 86; reaches Hangtown, 87
Wayman, Ruth (née Jones): 117; mother of John Hudson Wayman, 3 & n.
Wayman, Uncle Sol: 113
Wayman, Willard Gross: 3n., 22n., 119; 121 & n.; death, 22n.; guardian of Lizzie Jane Ormsby, 22n.; husband of Lizzie Jane Ormsby, 22n.
Wayman, Willard Ormsby: 22n.
Wayman, William: 3n., 115, 118
Weston, Mo.: 28, 29n.
Whitewater River: 76 & n.
Whitman, G.: 91, 93, 98 & n.
Willow Creek: 67 & n.
Wind River Mountains: 51n., 54n., 55 & n., 56
Wolf (Woolf) River: 30 & n.